atlanta

eat.shop atlanta
was researched, photographed and written
by agnes baddoo

01 toc
02 about
03 author notes
04 master list
05 neighborhood boundaries :
    getting around : map info
06 hotels
07 twenty favorites

11
13
15
17
19
21 bacchanalia
23 baraonda
25 belly general store
27 cabbagetown market and
    little's grill
29 carpe diem
31 carroll street cafe
33 chocolate pink pastry cafe
35 daddy d'z bbq
37 dakota blue
39 fat matt's rib shack /
    fat matt's chicken shack
41 floataway cafe
43 fritti
45 fune
47 hank's ice cream
49 highland bakery
51 krog bar
53 las palmeras
55 metrofresh
57 noir
59 nuevo laredo cantina
61 pacific kitchen
63 pangaea
65 paolo's gelato italiano
67 pearl restaurant and lounge
69 pleasant peasant
71 quinones at bacchanalia
73 r. thomas deluxe grill
75 rare
77 rathbun's
79 repast
81 ria's bluebird cafe
83 silver skillet restaurant
85 sotto sotto
87 souper jenny
89 southern sweets bakery
91 spoon
93 star provisions
95 stone soup kitchen
97 sun in my belly cafe
99 tierra
101 toast
103 toscano & sons italian market
105 wasabi
107 west egg cafe
109 zennubian 7 teahouse

123 city issue
125 dresscodes
127 eco-bella
129 elements of style
131 form
133 frock of ages
135 kaleidoscope boutique
    featuring 4 bags
137 knitch
139 little sparrow floral design
141 lui-b
143 luxe
145 mooncake
147 o'clair de lune
149 olive
151 pollen
153 providence antiques
155 savvy snoot
157 skate escape
159 south of market
161 sprout
163 standard
165 stefan's
167 the bilthouse
169 twelve boutique
171 twelve flowers
173 urban cottage
175 urban fusion
177 veruca
179 victoria's red carpet
181 victory vintage home
183 wiggle
185 young blood gallery &
    boutique

about eat.shop

the first thing to know about the *eat.shop guides* is that they are the only guides dedicated to featuring locally-owned eating and shopping establishments. the guides feature a fresh mix of places from posh to funky, spendy to thrifty, old school to just-opened, hip to under-the-radar. what do these places have in common? uniqueness, innovation and passion. you know these places weren't conceived out of a marketing plan, but out of someone's single-minded drive to create something special in their city.

the *eat.shop guides* feature approximately ninety carefully picked businesses. you may ask, why so few? because even though there are many good local businesses, we feature what we believe to be the great ones—the ones that are truly stand-outs. so if you only have a day or two to explore a city, we've happily done the leg work for you. or if you live in a city, an *eat.shop guide* is a quick and easy reference tool that can direct you to that fantastic new korean, hole-in-the-wall bbq place you've heard of or the bespoke milliner that's been in business for fifty years. and the best part? an *eat.shop guide* can be kept in your purse or messenger bag, or heck—even the floor of your car.

enough explaining, here are a couple of things to remember when using this guide:

• explore from neighborhood to neighborhood. note that almost every neighborhood featured has dozens of great stores and restaurants other than our favorites listed in this book. you'll find a listing of the neighborhoods, their street boundaries and the businesses within them on a following page.

• make sure to double check the hours of the business before you go by calling or visiting their website. often the businesses change their hours seasonally.

• the pictures and descriptions of each business are representational. please don't be distraught when the business no longer carries or is not serving something you saw or read about in the guide.

• at the *eat.shop guides*, the culture of a city is a major part of the experience. so whittle out some time to soak in the arts, the music, the architecture and even the street scene.

• if you're visiting the city, we know you'll need a rest eventually. so we've listed some of our favorite hotels to help you make your choice.

• the *eat.shop* clan consists of a small crew of creative types (ranging from graphic designer, to fashion stylist to a guy whose business is called "jon's awesome business") who travel extensively and have dedicated themselves to great eating and interesting shopping around the world. each of these people write, photograph and research their own books, and though they sometimes do not live in the city of the book they author, they draw from a vast network of local sources to deepen the well of information used to create the guides.

agnes's notes on atlanta

unlike other cities i have authored books in, atlanta is the first city i stepped blindly into—i was truly exploring new territory when i began work on *eat.shop atlanta*. but while i may have had no previous first-hand experience, numerous friends, as well as a wealth of music and film references put atlanta on my radar many years ago, and i've been fascinated since. when i finally met atlanta in person, it did not disappoint. for me, this city exudes the best of southern charm and hospitality crossed with urban sophistication. and there's something about the lushness of atlanta that made me fall in love completely—i now ask myself why it took me so long to get here—though everything happens when it's supposed to, right? so maybe all the years i have lived in l.a. driving around in circles not getting to where i wanted to go, but finding something better, came in handy before tackling this hilly green city where major streets arc, wind and twist north/south/east and west. for visitors that are used to an orderly grid of streets, you may need a bit of time to adjust, but never fear—you are never far from a peachtree something that will help orient you again.

other than the eating and the shopping which is fantastic, i offer you some of my other favorite things about this city:

1> **gardens and parks everywhere:** if you like green, atlanta is full of it. i note a number of parks in my features, as i just couldn't get enough of them. so take the time to sit, relax, decompress and digest.

2> **southern charm:** the gift of gab is apparent everywhere in this town. if you're visiting, don't hesitate to strike up a conversation with a local—they are born storytellers.

3> **the castleberry hills historic arts district:** culture is alive and well in atlanta in many different forms. visit this district which is bursting with energy and art, and don't miss the 4th friday art stroll.

4> **the carter center:** waging peace. fighting disease. building hope worldwide. go jimmy!

have a wonderful time exploring this vibrant city, i certainly did!

agnes baddoo
agnes@eatshopguides.com

the master list

castleberry hill historic arts district
eat:
noir
pearl restaurant and lounge
wasabi
zennubian 7 teahouse
shop:
o'clair de lune
urban fusion

westside midtown
eat:
bacchanalia
nuevo laredo cantina
pangaea
quinones at bacchanalia
spoon
star provisions
west egg cafe
shop:
1*five*0
belvedere
luxe
savvy snoot
sprout

downtown
eat:
pleasant peasant
rare

buckhead
eat:
antica posta
anis
souper jenny
shop:
beehive co-op
city issue
elements of style
olive
pollen
standard
the bilthouse
urban cottage
victoria's red carpet

emory university/ druid hills
eat:
floataway cafe

midtown
eat:
agnes & muriel's
baraonda
chocolate pink pastry cafe
fat matt's chicken shack/
fat matt's rib shack
fune
las palmeras
metrofresh
r. thomas deluxe grill
silver skillet restaurant
toast
tierra
shop:
fab'rik
lui-b
skate escape
twelve boutique
twelve flowers
veruca

virginia highland
eat:
belly general store
paolo's gelato italiano
shop:
20th century antiques
blabla
eco-bella
knitch
little sparrow floral design
mooncake
south of market

morningside
shop:
providence antiques

old 4th ward
eat:
highland bakery
repast

grant park
eat:
dakota blue
daddy d'z bbq
hank's ice cream
ria's bluebird cafe
stone soup kitchen
shop:
youngblood gallery and boutique

cabbagetown
eat:
agave
cabbagetown market and little's grill
carroll street cafe

inman park
eat:
11:11 teahouse
fritti
krog bar
pacific kitchen
rathbun's
sotto sotto

little five points/candler park/edgewood/historic kirkwood:
eat:
sun in my belly
shop:
form
frock of ages
stefan's

decatur
eat:
carpe diem
southern sweets bakery
shop:
dress codes
kaleidescope boutique featuring 4 bags
victory vintage home
wiggles

neighborhood boundaries : getting around : map info

castleberry hill historic arts district
walker street sw to peters street sw; mcdaniel street sw to spring street sw

westside midtown
marietta blvd. nw to howell mills road nw; west marietta street nw to chattahoochee avenue nw

downtown
centennial olympic park dr. nw to piedmont avenue ne; marietta street ne/edgewood avenue ne to north avenue

buckhead
northside drive to lenox road; lindbergh drive ne to piedmont road ne / roswell road ne

emory university/druid hills
fulton county line on the west, briarcliff rd. to the northwest, just over the emory rd. line on the north and following the southside of emory road

midtown
spring street to monroe drive; ponce de leon avenue ne to piedmont avenue

virginia highland
intersection of virginia avenue and north highland avenue; and side streets in each direction

morningside
piedmont avenue ne to highland avenue ne; amsterdam avenue ne to east morningside drive ne/ east rock springs road ne

old 4th ward
boulevard to randolph/glen iris; edgewood avenue to north avenue

grant park
hill street to boulevard; atlanta avenue to memorial drive

inman park
boulevard to moreland avenue ne; memorial drive to freedom parkway ne

cabbagetown
boulevard/carroll street ne to pearl street se; memorial drive se to wylie street se

little five points/candler park/edgewood/historic kirkwood
moreland avenue ne to harold avenue ne; memorial drive se to ponce de leon avenue ne

decatur
west ponce de leon/west trinity place to north arcadia avenue; east college avenue to north decatur road

directions and transportation

getting around atlanta requires more than just two feet and a good pair of shoes. it requires a car. there are scads of great options in the car rental market, but if you are in need a car to scoot around in for an hour or a full day — flexcar is a great choice.

flexcar is the alternative to the traditional way of renting — it saves time, money and is better for the environment because not only are you car-sharing, but the flexcar fleet consists of low emisson, fuel efficient vehicles. after purchasing a membership for a nominal fee, you simply reserve, pick up and drop off the car at one of numerous, convenient locations, and you're off!

check out flexcar.com to find out more. my travels around the city would just not have been the same without flexcar — thank you, thank you to liz wattenberg and ken for your kind support.*

a driving hint: peachtree is one of the main roads through town. it starts as a street, then turns into a road and then eventually a boulevard. you can take it from downtown, through midtown to buckhead (and beyond). if peachtree is trafficky, try piedmont avenue. and ponce de leon avenue is a good way to get to decatur.

maps

because we want to give you the most detailed maps possible, our city maps are now available online. please go to:

http://maps.eatshopguides.com/atlanta/

here you will find a map of the entire city, with indicators showing where each business is.

bookmark this url into your pda, and you'll have the mapping data right with you as you explore.

if you don't own a pda, but want a great street map of the city, the *eat.shop* authors love the *streetwise* maps. they are indispensable tools when you need a take-along map with lots of detail.

* the *eat.shop guides* partner with carefully selected travel companies that share the way we look at the world.

where to lay your weary head

there are many great places to stay in atlanta, but here are a few of my picks:

tea cakes bed and breakfast
1003 lena street nw
404.758.9879 www.atlantaluxuryinn.com
standard double from $110
notes: sumptuous b & b in a beautiful washington park location

the glenn hotel
110 marietta street nw
404.525.3739 www.glennhotel.com
standard double from $179
restaurant: glenn hotel restaurant + rooftop bar
notes: chic, downtown hotel with great package deals

the ellis hotel
176 peachtree street nw
404.523.5155 www.ellishotel.com
standard double from $150
restaurant: e street grill and lounge
notes: sophisticated boutique hotel in historic building downtown

indigo hotel atlanta
683 peachtree street ne
404.874.9200 www.hotelindigo.com
standard double from $175
restaurant: the golden bean
notes: stylish hotel opposite the fox theater in midtown

and a couple more suggestions:
w atlanta (www.starwoodhotels.com/whotels/atlanta)
twelve hotels (www.twelvehotels.com)

agnes's twenty favorite things

01 > sweet tea, ribs and mac 'n' cheese at agnes & muriel's
02 > ribs and smoked turkey at daddy d'z bbq
03 > almond apricot shortbread at southern sweets bakery
04 > bow tie pasta with fresh maine lobster at antica posta
05 > sunset sundae at hank's ice cream
06 > jasmine tears tea and visiting with penny at 11:11 teahouse
07 > drinks of any type at noir
08 > speck e rucola pizza at fritti
09 > rotisserie chicken at las palmeras
10 > shrimp po'boy at star provisions

11 > assia lingerie at o'clair de lune
12 > vintage raffia dress at frock of ages
13 > silver cart table at south of market
14 > missoni knits at luxe
15 > card catalog rolling coffee table at victory vintage home
16 > yves st. laurent green silk scarf at stefan's
17 > tasha hussey linen dress at beehive co-op
18 > chinese painted desk with bamboo trim at savvy snoot
19 > walter anderson woodcut prints at form
20 > faux bois at pollen

notes

notes

11:11 teahouse

calming teahouse

753 edgewood avenue. between waddell and spruce
404.521.1911 www.1111teahouse.com
daily 2 - 9p

opened in 2005. owner: penney sue barnes
$ - $$: all major credit cards accepted
tea. private tea parties. first come, first served

inman park > **e01**

part teahouse, part clubhouse, part arthouse—a trip to *11:11* can calm the nerves and soothe (or stimulate if you please) the senses. penney has a staggering assortment of teas to choose from here and she'll gladly share her knowledge of their healing properties should you be interested. or if you just need decompression, the light-filled front room beckons. if it's culture you're after, stop by in the evening, and chances are you'll find an art opening or some music being played and folks spilling out to the backyard, mingling 'round a cozy fire.

imbibe / devour:
penney's special blend
cardamom, ginger, red clover, nettle &
  black pepper blend
tangawizi (kenya black tea with ginger)
peony white needle
bao zhong oolong
jasmine tears green tea

agave

eclectic authentic southwestern eatery and tequila bar

242 boulevard southeast. corner of carroll street
404.588.0006 www.agaverestaurant.com
sun - thu 5 - 10p fri - sat 5 - 11p

opened in 2000. owner: jack sobel and tim pinkham chef: richard silvey
$ - $$: all major credit cards accepted
dinner. full bar. reservations recommended

cabbagetown > **e02**

if you have a hankering for the authentic flavors of new mexico, save the spendy airfare and look no further than *agave*. housed in a traditional adobe hacienda, *agave* sets the scene for all things hot, spicy and intensely flavorful. caution to those who are afraid of the heat: all peppers are represented in the cuisine here, from green chiles to chipotles. and with over 140 premium tequilas to choose from, rest assured the margarita of your dreams will do more than put out the fire.

imbibe / devour:
agave don eduardo anejo margarita on the rocks
herradura seleccion suprema tequila
smoked chicken quesadillas
southwestern shrimp & crab spring rolls
shrimp & sashimi tuna southwestern ceviche
chile rubbed pork over red chile puree & corn relish
ground veal, chorizo & green chile meatloaf
homemade chocolate mousse

agnes & muriel's

southern kitsch delicacies

1514 monroe drive northeast. between piedmont and cumberland
404.885.1000 www.mominthekitchen.com
mon - thu 11a - 10p fri 11a - 11p sat 10a - 11p sun 10a - 10p

opened in 1996. owner: david kitfield jr. chef: luther harris
$ - $$: all major credit cards accepted
brunch. lunch. dinner. coffee / tea. treats. beer / wine. first come, first served

midtown > **e03**

one step over the threshold of the cottage that houses *agnes & muriel's* and you're in pepto-pink and lime green '50s kitsch heaven. every nook and cranny is tastefully, yes, tastefully appointed with dolls and toys, '50s album covers and more ken and barbie scenarios than i ever knew existed. happy wait staff and smiling, satisfied patrons confirm what the glorious smells from the kitchen suggest: it may be fun out front, but luther don't play around when it comes to cooking. his southern treats here set the standard for hmm, hmm good.

imbibe / devour:
sweet tea (lord have mercy!)
mac n' cheese
coca cola bbq rib platter
fried chicken
skillet of fried green tomatoes
spinach crab cake salad
thanksgiving turkey sandwich
strawberry pound cake & whipped cream

15

anis

lively and authentic french bistro

2974 grandview avenue northeast. between pharr and peachtree
404.233.9889 www.anisbistro.com
lunch mon - sat 11:30a - 2:30p
dinner mon - sat 6 - 10p sun 6 - 9p

opened in 1994. owners: arnaud michel and jean-frederic perfettini chef: jeff gomez
$ - $$: all major credit cards accepted
lunch. dinner. full bar. reservations recommended

buckhead > **e04**

whenever i describe what kind of businesses are *eat.shop* type of businesses, i often use the description the "kind of their kind," meaning they do what they do better than anywhere else. *anis* is all you could want and more from a french country bistro. first there's the warm, *bon vivant* welcome followed by many french culinary favorites done to simple perfection. mix this with cozy, warmly colored rooms filled with antiques, art and mirrors and a patio surrounded by a bounty of flowers. add some occasionnal live music, *et voila*, provence in atlanta!

imbibe / devour:
côtes du rhône
pastis
mussels
farm house paté
free-range chicken with fingerling potatoes
beef tartar, capers & gauffre potatoes
filet mignon & grilled mushroom duxelle
profiterole

antica posta

ristorante toscano

529 east paces ferry road northeast. between maple and piedmont
404.262.7112 www.anticaposta.cpm
daily 4 - 11p

opened in 1999. owner: marco betti chefs: alessandro betti and enrico castanaza
$$: all major credit cards accepted
dinner. full bar. catering. private dining. reservations accepted

buckhead > e05

no matter how much fun i was having shooting *the bilt-house* down the street, i was driven to distraction by the aromas wafting my way from *antica posta*. thank goodness i didn't have to mind the store, and off i soon went to investigate *antica*. i was in for a treat. marco is the ambassador of tuscan cuisine in atlanta. bringing recipes from their sister restaurant in san casciano, italy, he and brother alessandro dazzle diners with their mouthwatering food. so loyal is their following that marco hosts yearly tours of tuscany for their faithful flock. if you feed them (well), they will follow!

imbibe / devour:
tignanello antinori (red wine)
cervaro della sala antinori (white wine)
seared scallops atop chickpea purée
tortelli stuffed with spinach & ricotta with duck ragu
homemade veal sausage with cannellini beans
piedmont ribeye steak on a bed of arugula
nougat ice cream cake

bacchanalia

contemporary american cuisine

1198 howell mill road northwest. corner of huff road
404.365.0410 www.starprovisions.com
mon - sat 6p - 9:30p

opened in 1993. chefs / owners: anne quatrano and clifford harrison
chef de cuisine: joshua hopkins
$$ - $$$: all major credit cards accepted
dinner. full bar. reservations recommended

westside midtown > e06

anne and clifford take to heart the slow food mission of lovingly produced, seasonal and local ingredients. besides being innovators in the atlanta culinary world at *bacchanalia*, they grow organic produce at their own summmerland farms with a number of their restaurant staffers helping to tend to the over sixty acres of herbs, raised bed agriculture and fruit and nut trees. back at *bacchanalia*, this intimate relationship with the ingredients translates to food that is infused with passion and care—and you'll taste it in every bite.

imbibe / devour:
05 albariño, campus stella, rias baixas
four-course prix fixe menu
texas gulf shrimp with gnocchi & preserved lemon
house-cured charcuterie
gulf crab fritter with thai pepper essence
orange creamsicle panna cotta with rhubarb
warm valrhona chocolate cake with mint ice cream

baraonda

caffé italiano

710 peachtree street. corner of third
404.879.9962 www.baraondaatlanta.com
mon - fri 11a - 10:30p sat 5p - midnight sun noon - 10p

opened in 2000. owners: mario maccarone and costanzo astarita
chef: costanza astarita   pizze chef: ferruccio cosenza
$ - $$: all major credit cards accepted
brunch. lunch. dinner. coffee / tea. treats. full bar
reservations accepted for parties of six or more

midtown > e07

baraonda is the perfect place for long, lazy lunches with friends after shopping. i envision the scene. we'd plop down, order the house cabernet, some antipasti for the table, a delectable pizze prosciutto di parma or pasta, and get down to dishing. we'd eat. then talk. drink, then talk. talk, then laugh. with all that chattering, we'll have made room for dessert. hail the tiramisu! a jolt of espresso and we'd be off! then again, maybe baraonda is also the perfect spot for long, lazy dinners with friends…

imbibe / devour:
baraonda california cabernet
salina prosecco with a splash of house limoncello
linguini con gameri
strozzapreti al cinghiale
pizze prosciutto di parma
pizze romana
cotolette d'agnello

23

belly general store

modern take on the traditional general store

772 north highland avenue northeast. corner of saint charles
404.872.1003 www.bellystore.com
mon - thu 7a - 5p fri - sat 7a - 7p sun 8a - 5p

opened in 2003. owner: melanie manning
$ - $$: all major credit cards accepted
breakfast. lunch. coffee / tea. treats. catering. gifts. first come, first served

virginia highland > e08

the name says it all: *belly general store*. here you'll find tasty treats to eat and also cool toys, antiques and objets that capture the imagination. whether it be a morning bagel and coffee, an obscure german candy or an old-fashioned wind-up toy, you'll find something that you want to eat or to own, or both, at this corner spot. as sweet and savory smells waft around the block, watch as a steady stream of folk makes its way into *belly* for a midday cupcake fix or to grab a gift and a sandwich.

imbibe / devour:
santander 100% espresso coffee
boylans cane cola
hand-made olive oil bagels
homestyle chicken salad sandwich
brownies & cupcakes
covet:
robot lilliput robot toy
antique vintage enamel plates

25

cabbagetown market and little's grill

a neighborhood grocery store, grill and deli

198 carroll street. between pickett and tennelle
404.221.9186 www.cabbagetownmarket.com
tue - fri 11a - 7p sat 11a - 8p sun noon - 6p

opened in 2007. owners: lisa hanson and maria locke
$: all major credit cards accepted
lunch. coffee / tea. treats. grocery. first come, first served

cabbagetown > e09

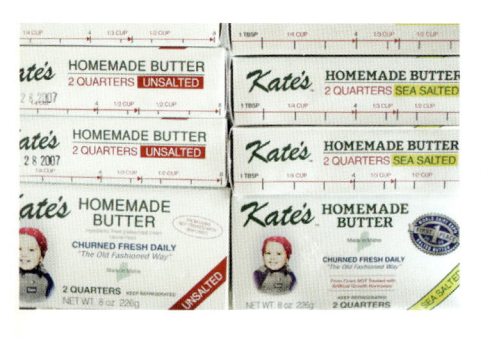

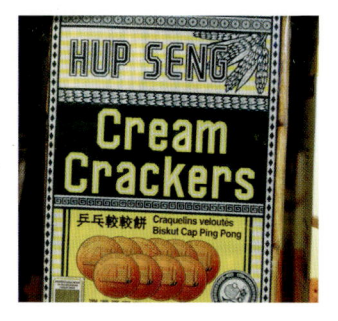

don't you just wish that every neighborhood had a small grocery teeming with healthy sundries and a counter grill serving fountain favorites like burgers? but wait, not just any old burgers, but locally raised, grass-fed beef burgers. thank you very much! in the shadow of the old fulton bag and cotton mill, lisa and maria resurrected a beloved neighborhood grocery and created the *cabbagetown market*—truly a convenient store for the modern day. with many of the original fixtures and sprucing up the inventory, it's all goodness and charm here in this little corner of cabbagetown.

imbibe / devour:
little's burger lime rickey
white oak pastures beefburger with pimento cheese
fried pickles
patak (local smoke house) hot dogs
sweetgrass dairy raw cow's milk cheese
glover farms grits & honey
local fresh farm eggs
10-cent mary janes!

27

carpe diem

international bistro, coffee house and lounge

105 sycamore place. near east college
404.687.9696 www.apresdiem.com
sun - thu 11a - midnight fri - sat 11 - 1a

opened in 2002. owner: andy alibakhsh chef: ciro ramos
$$: all major credit cards accepted
brunch. lunch. dinner. coffee / tea. treats. full bar
reservation accepted for parties of six or more

decatur > e10

the reason certain fads sweep a nation is usually because they're great ideas to begin with, though our country has practically super-sized three square meals into a death sentence which is not such a good idea. in contrast, some of the cuisines of europe and asia use small plates of food to balance out a meal. take tapas, for example. now there's a good idea. how can you go wrong with a variety of savory morsels? at *carpe diem,* tapas isn't a fad; it's a way of eating that makes sense. so seize the day, seize the menu and remember—variety is the spice of life!

imbibe / devour:
espresso doppio
pomegranate martini
mussels
niçoise salad
diver scallop tapas
brick-pressed roast beef sandwich
grilled marinated flank steak with chimichurri
chocolate fondant

carroll street cafe

historic neighborhood cafe

208 carroll street. corner of boulevard
404.577.2700 www.apresdiem.com
sun - thu 8a - midnight fri - sat 8a - 1ish

opened in 2002. owner: andy alibakhsh
$ - $$: all major credit cards accepted
breakfast. brunch. lunch. coffee / tea. full bar. first come, first served

cabbagetown > e11

while taking a shortcut from grant park to little five points, i wound up on a narrow, tiny street that instantly took me back in time to when the mills were still runnning in cabbagetown. what was once an area probably a bit bleak is now vibrant and bustling. amidst the brightly colored shingled houses and buildings jammed up next to one another, the *carroll street cafe* beckoned to me. detour! one south african sunrise later (tanqueray and limonata), i was sucked up into the *carroll street cafe* vortex and was happy to be there.

imbibe / devour:
terrapin beer company rye pale ale
south african sunrise
thai beef & tomato
escargot in garlic butter
betty sandwich
fig shiitake filet mignon
tropical tilapia
chocolate decadent cake

chocolate pink pastry café

french-style pastries and more

905 juniper street northeast, unit 108. corner of eighth
404.745.9292 www.chocolatepink.com
tues - thu 10a - 7p sun 10a - 7p fri - sat 10a - 11p

opened in 2006. owner: michael goodrich pastry chef: christian balbierer
$$: all major credit cards accepted
treats. coffee / tea. event room. reservations accepted on open table

midtown > e12

if you've ever played "tea party" as a child or with a child, the pastries from *chocolate pink* are what your imaginary tea party treats would be in real life: delicate, artful confections that barely make it from the box to the china. to avoid sticky fingers on the steering wheel (i couldn't wait to get home to eat the delights i had bought), treat yourself (and a real or imaginary friend) to a little tea party at the café— place napkin on lap, put pinky in the air while sipping your tea and indulge in a bit of sweet sustenance. this is one stylish place to indulge a sweet tooth.

imbibe / devour:
illy coffee & tea forte teas
cakes:
 petunia
 apple frangipane
 pineapple lemongrass
pink lemonade cupcake
wedding cakes & favors
norman love chocolates

daddy d'z bbq

the barbeque joint

264 memorial drive southeast. corner of hill
404.222.0206 www.daddydz.com
mon - fri 11a - 10:30p fri - sat 11a - midnight sun noon - 9:30p

opened in 1993. owner / grill master: ronnie newman
$: all major credit cards accepted
lunch. dinner. beer. live blues fri - sat night. first come, first served

grant park > e13

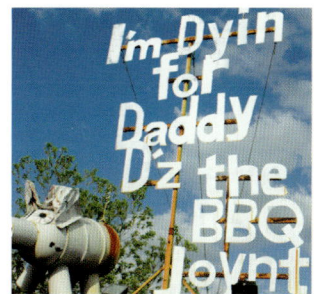

when i was in the band "the bushmills," one of our champions was george kilby, jr. renowned for his blues music and also for working with pinetop perkins, he is beloved for the southern hospitality he brought to our northern sensibilities with his monday night red beans and rice mixers. thanks to him, blues, bbq and beans (the holy trinity) are forever etched in my heart. *daddy d'z* makes me experience the trinity again. this place might be a bit of a dive, but mama, it dishes up smoky, cooked-all-day magic. it ain't pretty, but it's damn good!

imbibe / devour:
sweet tea
'bad to the bone' slab o' ribs
pit cooked 1/2 chicken & potato wedges
smoked turkey, collard greens & corn on the cob
red beans, rice & sausage
homemade brunswick stew
square of cornbread

dakota blue

a neighborhood joint
454 cherokee avenue. between memorial drive and sydney
404.589.8002
mon - fri 11:30a - 10p sat - sun 10a - 10p

opened in 2003. owners: alan and gigi conner
$: all major credit cards accepted
brunch. lunch. dinner. coffee / tea. treats. full bar. first come, first served

grant park > **e14**

although i do lots of prior research and have a daily schedule of businesses to visit, often when shooting these guides, things just catch my eye while i'm driving and i have to pull over and investigate. passing through grant park, i spied the twinkling lights and friendly chaos of *dakota blue*. i didn't even know i was hungry, but when i saw families and friends heartily enjoying one of the first al fresco-able nights of spring, it was all i needed to pull over and grab a bite. the power of suggestion in full force—and the scent of bacon cheeseburgers.

imbibe / devour:
red stripe
mimosa
bacon cheeseburger
black bean cuban sandwich
corn dogs & fries ("without all that carny attitude!")
pulled pork sandwich
two tacos del carnivore
apple pie a la mode

fat matt's rib shack /
fat matt's chicken shack

bbq and blues

1821 piedmont avenue northeast. near montgomery ferry
rib: 404.607.1622 / chicken: 404.875.2722 www.fatmattsribshack.com
see website for hours

opened in 1990. owners: matt and kelly harper
$ - $$: mc. visa
lunch. dinner. beer. catering. first come, first served

midtown > **e15**

somehow it just ain't bbq unless it's off the side of the road and there's some swingin' down home blues involved. but let's not forget that bbq is not just ribs. the bird must be honored as well. *fat matt's* has done just that with two shacks sitting side by side that pay homage to both the pig and the bird. the chicken shack is smaller and it features soul food: fried chicken or fish with greens while the rib shack next door serves up smokedhits from the pit and dishes up live blues on the side. so good, like l'il richard would say: "it makes my big toe shoot up in my boot!"

imbibe / devour:
lemonade
iced tea
fried chicken
full slab of ribs
rum baked beans
pulled pork sandwich
sweet potato soufflé

39

floataway cafe

california-inspired mediterranean and italian cuisine
1123 zonolite road northeast, suite 15. off johnson road
404.892.1414 www.starprovisions.com
tue - sat 6p - whenever

opened in 1998. owners / chefs: anne quatrano and clifford harrison
chef de cuisine: drew belline
$$: all major credit cards accepted
dinner. full bar. reservations accepted for parties of two or more

virginia · highland > **e16**

over the river and through the woods, to the far end of an industrial park i go, lies a comfortable, modern cafe where space and time truly do stand still. *floataway* is where the fine folks from *bacchanalia*, clifford and anne, create lovely, fresh cuisine with a california-mediterranean twist. in some ways, the *floataway* is not really a cafe, though it's certainly not a formal restaurant either. what's enticing is the menu's simplicity. it has a homey twist to it that makes everything plate-licking good.

imbibe / devour:
mint julep
floataway daiquiri on the rocks
harney & sons hibiscus tea
ribolita of cannellini beans, ceci peas & greens
fried soft shell crabs & pommes frites
pan-roasted skate wing with lemon & herbs
soft-serve ice cream with extra virgin olive oil &
   fleur de sel

fritti

authentic neopolitan pizzas and light southern italian fare

309 north highland avenue. corner of elizabeth
404.880.9559 www.frittirestaurant.com
lunch mon - fri 11:30a - 3p sat 11:30a - 4p sun 1 - 4p
dinner mon - thu 5:30 - 11p fri 5:30 - midnight sat 4 - midnight sun 4 - 10p

opened in 2000. owner / chef: riccardo ullio
$ - $$: all major credit cards accepted
lunch. dinner. full bar. reservations recommended

inman park > **e17**

cholesterol be damned—name a restaurant *fritti* and i'm all over it! start here with some of the namesake fritti: little fried veggies or fruits of the sea. then have a salad, and then order a certified neopolitan pizza. yep, certified. you only get this recognition after receiving strict training and then adhering to the culinary discipline of the "associazione verace pizza." phew. thankfully, riccardo knows what goes into such strict guidelines and we, the eaters, never have to concern ourselves with such tediousness. instead, just dig in and enjoy!

imbibe / devour:
negroni
milano
bresaola della valtellina
arrancini
pancetta e cipolla pizza
speck e rucola pizza
funghi di bosco pizza

fune

sushi bar, ultra lounge
860 peachtree street northeast. corner of seventh
404.541.9322 www.funesushibar.com
lunch mon - fri 11:30a - 2:30p dinner sun - sat 5 - 11p

opened in 2007. owner: david kim chef: tim dumansky
$$: all major credit cards accepted
lunch. dinner. full bar. reservations recommended

midtown > **e18**

fune is more than these things: more than cleverly named, tasty cocktails. more than gorgeously presented sushi rolling by on a conveyor belt. more than tim's ridiculously delicious japanese-inspired entrees. fune is also an architectural marvel. an awe-inspiring room that showcases all of the above. it's a sexy slice of modern tokyo in atlanta. and twelve flowers' inspired floral arrangements add the finishing touch to an experience that satisfies all the senses.

imbibe / devour:
"our" cosmo
green tea sake-tini
white snow roll
crazy monkey roll
jumbo lump crab cakes with asparagus &
  lobster scallion rice cake
beef tenderloin medallions

hank's ice cream

classic homemade ice cream parlour
5658 riverdale road. at flat shoals
770.907.5813   www.hanksicecream.com
tue - sun 2 - 9p

opened in 2003. owner: douglas wiggins
$: cash
treats. first come, first served

college park > **e19**

some of my fondest childhood memories involve going for after=dinner walks on central park west in manhattan to get an ice cream. when i arrived at *hank's ice cream* one friday around dusk, i was awash in sweet nostalgia. it was like déjà vu. and though we only feature locally owned businesses in these guides—we are going to make an exception for *hank's*, as this is the atlanta outpost of the houston original. how could we not include this family-run place that serves flavors like banana pudding?

imbibe / devour:
ice cream:
  rose petal
  pineapple upside-down cake
  black walnut
sorbet:
  mango chili rub
  guava
  tamarind

47

highland bakery

beloved bake shop and restaurant

655 highland avenue northeast, suite 10. between sampson and glen iris
404.586.0772 www.highlandbakery.com
mon - fri 7a - 4p sat - sun 8a - 4p

opened in 2003. owner: stacey eames sugar artist: karen portaleo
$ - $$: all major credit cards accepted
breakfast. lunch. brunch. coffee / tea. treats. catering. first come, first served

cabbagetown / old fourth ward > **e20**

there's a lot going on in the old factory that houses *highland bakery*. besides a great breakfast and lunch menu, there's the imported-from-germany stone mill. watch in wonder as the wheat goes through it; feel as if you're watching some of the secrets of the universe being answered. and what comes out of the mill goes into the cooking and baking on-site, including sugar artist karen's amazing confections. she can concoct anything out of sugar and flour that you can imagine. and based on some of the spectacular creations, imaginations run big around here.

imbibe / devour:
batdorf & bronson coffee
house-blend iced tea
sweet potato pancakes
crab cakes benedict
stone ground (on site) honey wheat bread
highland white chili - yum!
seven-layer strawberries & cream cake
karen's extraordinary creative confections

krog bar

mediterranean-inspired small plates bar

112 krog street northeast. corner of lake
404.524.1618 www.krogbar.com
mon - sat 4:30 - midnight

opened in 2005. owners: kevin rathbun, cliff bramble and kirk parks
chef: kevin rathbun chef de cuisine: jonathon allen
$$: all major credit cards accepted
light dinner. wine / beer. first come, first served

inman park > e21

sometimes i can be overcome with spells of indecisiveness. this might have something to do with my zodiac chart, or it might be something much simpler—i can't make up my mind because i like more than one thing. this is one of the reasons i love *krog bar*. here i can select several small plates of mediterranean-inspired treats. and i know i will start with the bresaola as it's one of my all-time favorite cured meats. any opportunity to indulge in this is one fewer moments of indecision. hmm, what to have next?

imbibe / devour:
02 vina rey crianza
xarmant txakoli
bresaola
fig almond cake
prosciutto & roasted pepper tramezzi
ahi tuna with sun-dried apricot vinegar
capra cremosa with black truffle
piedras de chocolate

las palmeras

authentic cuban food

368 fifth street. corner of duran
404.872.0846
wed - fri 11:30a - 3p 5:30 - 9:45p sat noon - 9:45p

opened in 1992. owners: felipe and maida alvarez chef: maida alvarez
$: all major credit cards accepted
lunch. dinner. beer / wine. first come, first served

midtown > e22

smack-dab in the middle of a lush, tree-lined residential street, felipe and maida serve up their cuban family favorites at *las palmeras*. one of the reasons i love cuban food is because it's not too fussy or mysterious—there are no sauces with overly complex flavors nor the use of heart attack-inducing spices. *las palmeras* feels just right, with its laid-back warmth and simplicity. from felipe's built-by-hand patio to maida's marinated sloooow roasted pig or bird or beef, char-grilled and caramelized perfection—this family has the touch to make you feel right at home!

imbibe / devour:
cuban coffee
materva yerba mate soda
felipe's rotisserie chicken
puerco asado
veggie plate
pollo frito
ropo viejo
guava shells

metrofresh

fresh food fast

931 monroe drive northeast. corner of ninth street
404.724.0155 www.metrofreshatl.com
mon - fri 7 - 9:30a mon - sat 11a - 9p sun 10a - 3p

opened in 2006. owner and chef: mitchell anderson
$ - $$: all major credit cards accepted
breakfast. brunch. lunch. dinner. treats. first come, first served

midtown > e23

all around the world, chicken soup = comfort. that's why mitchell (a protégé of *souper jenny*) always has at least one kind of chicken soup (as well as his signature chili) on his menu at *metrofresh*. when you think about it, everything made here is about comforting you with the most satisfying and healthy foods possible, made out of the freshest ingredients and influenced by flavors from around the world. the only thing fast about this fast food is that everything is always ready to go.

imbibe / devour:
metrofreshual blend fresh ground coffee
hot cereal of the day
thai coconut chicken soup with rice
mitchili
phenomenal tomato & mint salad with
  walnuts, chilis & pomegranate dressing
london broil sandwich
lobster tacos

noir

old hollywood-inspired bar and lounge

264 peters street southwest. between fair and mcdaniel
404.223.2999 www.noiratlanta.com
tue - sat 8p - late

opened in 2007. owner: jason gabriel wertz chef: omar powell
$ - $$: all major credit cards accepted
small plates. full bar. first come, first served

castleberry hill arts district > **e24**

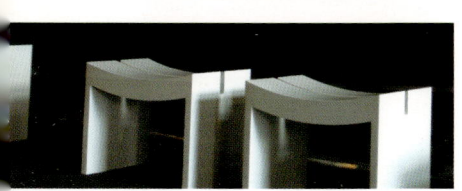

film noir is about plot twists, moody atmosphere and above all, style. with its plush black, white, and red velvet décor, *noir* sets a sultry mood. no matter what kind of hectic day you've had in the outside world, one phantom lady and you'll be seeing everything in black and white, speaking like you're in a bogart and bacall flick—though you may be influenced by one of the films projecting on the brick wall more than the drink. *noir* is more than just cocktails—it's about old-world charm, civility and conversation. the perfect way to end a day of gallery hopping.

imbibe / devour:
the phantom lady
naked kiss
cafés richard grand cru estate coffee
tomato napolean with tapanade, basil & parsley
arugula salad with almonds & strawberries
shrimp noir
spaghetti squash & green onion fritter

nuevo laredo cantina

home-cooked mexican food

1495 chattahoochee avenue northwest. between hills and marieta
404.352.9009 www.nuevolaredocantina.com
mon - thu 11a - 10p fri - sat 11a - 11p

opened in 1991. owner: chance evans
$: all major credit cards accepted
lunch. dinner. full bar. reservations accepted for parties of six or more

westside midtown > **e25**

bonnie raitt sings, "your sweet and shiny eyes are like the stars above laredo, like meat and potatoes, to me." this is what chance must've been singing to himself when he discovered mexican homecooking while based in mexico city over forty years ago. so much so that he opened the plucked-from-a-border-town-style *nuevo laredo cantina* here in atlanta where he keeps the menu basic, but oh-so delicious. "in my sweet dreams we are in a bar and it's my birthday, drinking salty margaritas with fernando." i haven't seen fernando, but the margaritas here are out of this world!

imbibe / devour:
house margarita
cadillac margarita
panchos
fresh avocado taco with cheese
brisket barbacoa
chicken taco & enchilada with rice & beans
caldo de pollo
flan

pacific kitchen

intimate and ambient california-inspired restaurant

913 bernina avenue northeast. corner of north highland
404.223.9292 www.pacific-kitchen.com
brunch sun 11a - 3p
tue - thu 5 - 10p fri - sat 5 - 11p sun 5 - 9:30p

opened in 2006. owner: kelly fueschel chef: nick leahy pastry chef: kelly fueschel
$$: all major credit cards accepted
brunch. dinner. full bar. reservations accepted for parties of four or more

inman park > e26

pacific kitchen sits perched in a house on a hill, overlooking a picturesque park. the setting and the vibe immediately made me feel like i was in northern california. and then when i perused the menu, i wondered if i had inadvertently clicked my heels together three times, magically transporting me to the golden state. nick creates wondrous dishes here with fresh pacific seafood and kelly's mouth-watering dessert concoctions are as beautiful as they are delicious. california dreaming on a sunny atlanta day.

imbibe / devour:
black pepper corn martini
stormhoek pinotage, south africa
sweet tasmanian crab & corn fritters
grilled ostrich filet with sautéed fava beans
grilled island spice pork medallions with
  yellow rice, chorizo & spring peas
butter-poached lobster ravioli
miniature dessert trio

pangaea

delicious global grub

1082 huff road. between howell mills and 14th
404.350.8787 www.globalgrubbin.com
brunch sat 9a - 2p
mon - fri 11a - 3p sat 11a - 4p

opened in 2002. owners: butch and pam raphael chef: butch raphael
$: all major credit cards accepted
lunch. brunch. coffee / tea. treats. catering. first come, first served

westside midtown > **e27**

young and old, far and wide, people told me that *pangaea* was one of their fave atlanta eating spots. and even though i had it on my must-do list, i ended up there on a day i was headed somewhere else. no matter because just as the sky was opening up for a spring drenching, i hungrily happened upon *pangaea*. i threw my previous plan aside and took the opportunity to explore the thinking behind *pangaea*. 'pan' means bread in many languages and 'gaea' means fresh ingredients from the earth. sounds good to me. and tastes even better.

imbibe / devour:
jasmine green iced tea
blackberry lemonade
grilled veggies
grilled pacific rim salmon salad
chicken banh mi sandwich
lemongrass pork noodle bowl
almond joy brownie

63

paolo's gelato italiano

traditional, yet innovative italian gelato

1025 virginia avenue northeast. corner of highland
404.607.0055 www.paolosgelato.com

opened in 1999. owner / chef: paolo dalla zorza
$: cash only
treats. coffee. first come, first served

virgina · highland > **e28**

paolo is a slightly mad, frozen-treats professor—a gelato genius if you will. just ask some of the gelato purveyors in the country; they all agree on paolo's inventiveness. it's not only his spectacular variety of flavors, it's his passion for quality that makes him the maestro di gelato. from offering classes in traditional italian gelato-making to designing and wholesaling products like a lucite-handled spatula to better scoop your gelato with, this guy has all the bases covered. grazie paolo!

imbibe / devour:
gelato:
  rose
  basil
  olive oil
  caffe & hazelnut
  proseco
cannoli
non-dairy gelato for your pet!

65

pearl restaurant & lounge

both lounge and fine dining
253 peters street southwest. between fair and mcdaniel
404.523.2121
mon - thu 4p - midnight fri - sat 4p - 2a sun 2 - 10p

opened in 2006. owner / chef: dishema fulton
$ - $$: all major credit cards accepted
dinner. coffee / tea. treats. full bar. reservations accepted for parties of six or more

castleberry hill arts district > e29

here's the what's up with *pearl restaurant & lounge*: it's cool, it's modern and airy, and it has a very cocktail-esque atmosphere. but let's set the record straight because everybody knows *pearl* is truly about the crab! and the lobster! and the peel-and-eat shrimp! so *pearl* is as much a fantastic dining destination as it is a chic lounge. and if the menu looks familiar, it's because *pearl* is the better-dressed sibling of *baltimore crab & seafood* where you can grab much of the same great food for take-out.

imbibe / devour:
indaba chenin blanc, south africa
pear punch
sweet tea
garlic blue crabs & corn on the cob
fried tilapia sandwich
grilled salmon salad
peel-and-eat shrimp
banana pudding

pleasant peasant

inspired interpretations of classic french fare

55 peachtree street northeast. coroner of linden
404.874.3223 www.thepeasantrestaurants.com
brunch sat - sun 11a - 3p lunch mon - fri 11:30a - 2:30p
dinner sun - thu 5 - 10p fri - sat 5 - 11p

opened in 1973. owners: pam furr and maureen kalmansan chef: david gross
$ - $$: all major credit cards accepted
lunch. dinner. brunch. full bar. reservations accepted for parties of six or more

downtown > e30

the *pleasant peasant* is a pioneer. it was the first restaurant in atlanta to serve nouvelle cuisine. most of us had never even heard of this type of cuisine until the '80s, but the *pleasant peasant* started dishing it up in 1973 and has been wowing diners ever since with their twist on french country fare. it has a romantically rustic feel here, and whether you're wearing jeans or a tux (or both), you'll feel comfortable. in a world where many restaurants struggle to survive, it's a pleasure to dine at a place that has defied all odds and has not only survived but become legendary.

imbibe / devour:
fat bastard, chardonnay, france
mad fish, shiraz, australia
marinated chicken livers
young harris trout
plum pork
shrimp villages
chocolate intemperance
strawberry shortcake

69

quinones at bacchanalia

super-fine dining
1198 howell mill road. corner of huff
404.365.0410 www.starprovisions.com
tue - sat 6p - whenever

opened in 2005. chefs / owners: anne quatrano and clifford harrison
chef de cuisine: david carson
$$$: all major credit cards accepted
dinner. full bar. private parties. reservations recommended

westside midtown > **e31**

entering *quinones*, i half expected a flourish of trumpets to announce my arrival. i was immediately transfixed by the opulent surroundings and felt like i had morphed into cinderella at the ball well before midnight. i looked down to see if i was wearing glass slippers. i wasn't. phew. no evil stepmother or threat of pumpkin chariots to ruin what i expected to be an extraordinary dining experience. *quinones* is where anne and clifford bring fantasy to the table. and i suggest that you give yourself over fully to this flight of fancy.

---

imbibe / devour:
créme de cassis with prosecco
poached fanny bay oysters in a green garlic & ramp stew
carolina squab with baby fennel, potato dumplings & wild onions
wild virginia black bass with english peas & fava bean succotash
strawberry popsicle & black pepper ice cream

r. thomas' deluxe grill

healthy, eclectic american diner

1812 peachtree street northwest. between 26th and 28th
404.872.2942 www.rthomasdeluxegrill.com
24/7. 365 days a year

opened in 1985. owners: richard and jim thomas chef: donna gate (nutritionist)
$ - $$: all major credit cards accepted
breakfast. brunch. lunch. dinner. coffee / tea. treats. beer / wine
first come, first served

midtown > e32

thanks to richard and *r. thomas' deluxe grill*, greasy spoons no longer have the monopoly on late-night dining. that's right. if you're hungry in the middle of the night, or any time for that matter, you can now have tasty and healthy organic food: vegetarian and vegan options, a classic burger or bacon and eggs. yes, i said bacon, folks. vegans and carnivores can finally dine together and neither will be shunned for his or her choices. and if you're here in the daytime, no visit is complete without seeing richard's birds and garden— they are the inspiration for his "food for life" revolution.

imbibe / devour:
lady bug
donkey kong smoothie
r. thomas' burger
organic grilled soy ginger salmon with quinoa
raw walnut sunflower pâté with raw guacamole
the down home
sloppy veggie joe
turtledove cheesecake

rare

tapas soul restaurant
354a piedmont avenue. between renaissance and linden
404.541.0665 www.rareatl.com
mon - thu 5p - midnight fri - sat 5p - 1a sun noon - 5p

opened in 2006. owner: lorenzo wyche chef: anthony sanders
$$: all major credit cards accepted
dinner. full bar. reservations recommended

downtown > e33

in the south, the gift of gab seems to be something fortified in the water, so any good drinking hole is going to be more than just a place for boozin'— there's also the schmoozin' to consider. at *rare*, you and your posse can curl up on day beds, kick back and let the festivities begin. colorful cocktails serve to fuel the fun, but it's anthony's soul food tapas, inspired by his grandmother coretha's famous recipes, that really get the tongues a-waggin'!

imbibe / devour:
black & blue cocktail
pomnac
collard green potsickers
hoppin' john risotto with shrimp & scallions
jerk style tilapia with sweet plantains & lime nage
forever braised baby back ribs
loiusiana crawfish & steak pot pie
flaming bananas foster over pound cake

rathbun's

edgy peasant (new american) food

112 krog street northeast. corner of lake
404.524.8280 www.rathbunsrestaurant.com
mon - thu 5:30 - 10:30p fri - sat 5:30 - 11:30p

opened in 2004. owner / chef: kevin rathbun pastry chef: kirk parks
$$: all major credit cards accepted
dinner. full bar. private parties. cooking classes. reservations recommended

inman park > **e34**

bring out the big guns because kevin is not foolin' around at the restaurant that sports his last name: *rathbun's*. if you're looking for frilly delicacies, bye-bye. if you're up to a caloric commitment, then hello! what do i mean by this? well, for me, any entree involving bone marrow, fleur de sel and butter brioche is a "diet be damned, eat, drink and be merry" proposition that i'll gladly accept. and when there's a course called the second mortgage, just excuse me while i call my banker and confirm that i can afford to move on in to devour without guilt.

imbibe / devour:
gruatini
macallan cask strength scotch whiskey
roasted bone marrow, fleur de sel & butter brioche
lump crab tart with creole mustard
the second mortgage:
　maine lobster & roasted green chile soft taco
fuji apple cobbler & sage ice cream
banana peanut butter cream pie

77

repast

foreward-thinking american bistro with world influences

620 glen iris drive northeast. corner of north
404.870.8707 www.repastrestaurant.com
mon - sat 5:30 - 10:30p

opened in 2006. owners / chefs: joe truex and mihiko obunai
$$: all major credit cards accepted
dinner. full bar. private parties. cooking classes
reservations accepted for parties of six or more

old fourth ward > **e35**

what do you get when you put together classical french training, japanese macrobiotic and raw food interests and a bit of louisiana cooking? you get joe and mihiko and what is created when you marry their diverse backgrounds and passions: *repast*. where else in this town could you find a menu that dares to meld octopus, vidalia onions and watermelon?. nowhere, except the refreshing and exciting *repast*. take the journey here; you won't regret the experience.

imbibe / devour:
repastini
apple cider martini
sugar cane skewered scallops with mango salad
tomato fennel soup & mini grilled cheese
mihiko's daily macrobiotic composition
sweetbread & wild escargot terrine
chorizo-crusted heritage pork chop,
 swiss chard & candied sweet potatoes

ria's bluebird cafe

beloved all-day breakfast and lunch spot

421 memorial drive southeast. corner of cherokee
404.521.3737 www.riasbluebird.com
daily 8a - 3p

opened in 2000. owners: ria pell and alexander skalicky chef: ria pell
$: mc. visa
breakfast. lunch. brunch. coffee/tea. treats. first come, first served

grant park > **e36**

it was a lazy sleep-in sunday, on an unusually cold and rainy april morning. where should we go for brunch? saturn's suggestion—*ria's bluebird* for the pancakes. "you mean, the caramelized banana ones?" asked saturn's mom, marcia. "whatever, mom." eyeroll. so off we went. i usually hate brunch "out" because of the crowds and lines, but *ria's* had that cozy bed-head variety of both, and somehow neither bothered me. and then there are the pancakes. saturn hit the banana ones first, then marcia's fork ventured forth, and then mine. "hey, mom! leave my pancakes alone!"

imbibe / devour:
homemade lemonade
fresh o.j.
buttermilk pancakes
country-fried tempeh with gravy, grilled tomato
 & sautéed spinach on a grilled biscuit
bbq brisket
pepper turkey melt

81

silver skillet restaurant

classic southern diner

200 fourteenth street northwest. corner of fowler
404.874.1388
mon - fri 6:30a - 2:30p sat - sun 8a - 2p

opened in 1956. owner: theresa breckinridge
$: all major credit cards accepted
breakfast. lunch. first come, first served

midtown > **e37**

little feat sings a song where they say, "oh atlanta, i've got to get back to you!" one of the things that little feat must have wanted to get back to was the *silver skillet*. this place is a tried-and-true, worn but not weary, busy all day, old-school southern diner. this is where you get your biscuits n' gravy, pork chops and mash, fried chicken, peach cobbler, waitresses who call you "hon" and breakfast all day long. the *silver skillet* is a time capsule on a platter, the south in your mouth and a place i can't wait to get back to!

imbibe / devour:
sweet tea
baked chicken with sweet potato & black-eyed peas
fried chicken, mashed potatoes & gravy
open-faced roast beef sandwich
scrambled eggs, bacon & biscuits
corn bread
peach cobbler
ice box lemon pie

83

sotto sotto

cucina italiana

313 north highland avenue. corner of elizabeth
404.523.6678 www.sottosottorestaurant.com
open daily for dinner at 5:30p

opened in 1999. owner / chef: riccardo ullio
$ - $$: all major credit cards accepted
dinner. treats. full bar. reservations recommended

inman park > **e38**

one forkful into my *polletto al limone* at *sotto sotto* and i want to hang a sign around my neck that says, "do not disturb." conversation, however idle, i'm sure would be more distraction than i can bear. one mouthful of this savory and tender chicken, and all my senses are focused. is it the flavor that's so entrancing? or maybe the divine aroma? i don't know, but i'm going to keep eating. this must be a common reaction to the food here because the bar is full with diners seemingly absorbed in a culinary bliss that could only be described as, well... private.

imbibe / devour:
limoncello cosmopolitan
sunkissed godmother
assagio d'olio
bresaola di tonno
tortelli di erbette
risotto mantecato
pesce arrosto
polletto al limone

85

souper jenny

100% homemade soups

56 east andrews drive, #22. between paces ferry and cains hill
404.239.9023 www.souperjennyatl.net
mon - fri 11a - 5p sat 11a - 4p sun 10a - 3p

opened in 1999. owner / chef: jenny levison
$: cash
lunch. classes. first come, first served

buckhead > **e39**

in case you hadn't figured it out, soup is jenny's "thing." and judging by the continuous line from opening 'til closing at *souper jenny*, her soup is everybody's thing. and now it's my thing, too. while enjoying a bowl of green soup here, i was looking around the sunny, marigold-colored surroundings and i was drawn to watching the little people area. there's an alcove with kids' tables so the young'uns can sit amoung themselves enjoying healthy, homey treats, discussing the things that matter to them the most. like, "when's the brownie course?"

imbibe / devour:
souper-powered green! soup
mango gazpacho
my dad's turkey chili
chicken tortilla wrap
homemade pita stuffed with lucia's chicken salad
ginger sesame salad
wheatberry salad
make your own s'mores

southern sweets bakery

family-run bakery and cafe

186 rio circle. corner of laredo
404.373.8752 www.southernsweets.com
mon - fri 9a - 6p sat 11a - 6p

opened in 1992. owner / chef: nancy cole head baker: fahra kriskovic
$ - $$: all major credit cards accepted
lunch. coffee / tea. treats. catering. first come, first served

decatur > **e40**

after crossing a railroad track (twice!) and driving literally hill and dale, i arrived at an industrial park that i was not sure was still within atlanta city limits. alas, it was. the moment i opened the car door, i was overcome by the intoxicating scent wafting out of the *southern sweets bakery*, and nothing else mattered except for following the scent. the flurry of on-their-way-home-from-work customers scurrying in right up 'til closing time here confirmed what i already knew: when it comes to sugar and butter, there are no hurdles that will keep us from getting to the prize.

imbibe / devour:
different pimento cheese sandwich
spicy turkey sausage gumbo
roast turkey club
almond apricot shortbread
pecan tarte
carrot spice cake
ginger shortbread cookies
old-fashioned chocolate layer cake

spoon

authentic thai cuisine

758 marietta street northwest, suite a. corner of means
404.522.5655 www.spoonatl.com
mon - fri 11a - 11p sat 4 - 11p sun reserved for private parties

opened in 2005. owners: sujaree suteeluxnaporn and aim suteeluxnaporn
chef: aim suteeluxnaporn
$ - $$: all major credit cards accepted
lunch. dinner. full bar. reservations recommended

westside midtown > **e41**

how do i love *spoon*? let me count the ways: i love the spacious, yet still inviting surroundings. i love that the traditional thai recipes here have a twist to them, thanks to the innovation of chef aim. i love that the food is incredibly flavorful but not too tongue-numbingly hot. and i love the desserts. i will say this again for emphasis: i love the desserts. this is the area on the menu where my spoon really got a workout. the carrot cake with cinnamon ice cream was a taste sensation and revelation. my mouth waters just thinking about it.

imbibe / devour:
spoon martini
pomegranate martini
basil roll
nam tok beef salad
golden red snapper
pad kra prao
dungeness crab pad cha
lemongrass panna cotta with tamarind sorbet

star provisions

a cook's marketplace

1198 howell mill road. corner of huff
404.365.8020 www.starprovisions.com
mon - sat 10a - 10p

opened in 1999. owners: clifford harrison and anne s. quatrano
$$: all major credit cards accepted
breakfast. brunch. lunch. dinner. coffee / tea. treats. beer / wine
first come, first served

westside midtown > e42

i am a sucker for culinary supply stores. so, on principle alone, i was sucked right into *star provisions*. more than a general store, this is a culinary department store of galactic proportions with an abundance of beautiful kitchen and housewares, the finest of meats and house-cured charcuterie, fresh fish, obscure cheeses, and wines (of which many appear on the menus at anne and clifford's restaurants). not kitchen inclined? not to worry—the extensive variety of prepared foods and baked goods assure that you won't go hungry. so everybody is a star here.

imbibe / devour:
victorian lemonade with ginger & herbal extracts
clochette goats milk cheese
shrimp po' boy
asparagus sandwich with serrano ham
chicken pot pie
covet:
angela adams spike rug
bamboo picnicware

93

stone soup kitchen

food you'd be fixin' at home if you had time to fix it

584 woodward avenue. between boulevard and park
404.524.1222 www.stonesoupkitchen.net
mon - fri 6:30a - 3p sat - sun 9a - 3p

opened in 2005. owner: sarah rick
$: all major credit cards accepted
breakfast. brunch. lunch. dinner. coffee / tea. treats. beer / wine
first come, first served

cabbagetown / grant park > e43

i love music and i love food. i've created little soundtracks that play in my mind when i think of some of the businesses that i've visited while working on this book. when lisa from *cabbagetown market* raved to me about this place, i hopped into my car singing, "hurry down to the *stone soup kitchen*." i re-worked laura nyro's "stoned soul picnic" which is a song that uses the word "surry" in it. i don't know what "surry" means, so i changed the lyric to hurry, and y'all know what hurry means. so follow my lead and hurry down here to see what sarah's got on her delicious menu.

imbibe / devour:
iced dancing goat coffee
cuban black bean soup
buttermilk pancakes
red mule grits
  (ground in athens by a mule named luke)
lil's favorite sandwich
buzz boy club
julie b's peach cobbler

sun in my belly

quintessential european neighborhood cafes

neighborhood cafe: 2161 college avenue northeast. corner of murray hill
garden cafe: 1345 piedmont road. at the atlanta botanical garden
nc: 404.370.1088 / gc: 404.532.7375 www.suninmybelly.com
mon - sat 8a - 9p sun 9a - 9p

opened in 1998. owners: max leblanc and alison lueker chef: alison lueker
$ - $$: all major credit cards accepted
breakfast. jazz brunch. lunch. dinner. coffee / tea. treats. catering. events
first come, first served (reservations needed for supper club)

historic kirkwood / atlanta botanical garden > **e44**

the phrase "sun in my belly" conjures up such a giddy, glowing feeling. i am happy to report that *sun in my belly*, the sweet neighborhood cafe in kirkwood, manages to meet and surpass this sentiment. in the restored hardware store that the cafe is housed in, alison re-invigorates classics that pack a flavor wallop. her food is so yummy and the space so welcoming, you best throw out your schedule for the rest of the day and just lazily hang-out with a warm and happy glow inside your belly.

imbibe / devour:
espresso
kirkwood breakfast
classic blt with hash browns
napoleon complex panini
classic southern mac 'n' cheese
venus salad
supper club prix fixe three- course menu
gingerbread pound cake

tierra

flavors of the americas

1425b piedmont avenue northeast. corner of westminster
404.874.5951 www.tierrarestaurant.com
tue - thu 6 - 10p fri - sat 6 - 10:30p

opened in 1999. owners / chefs: dan and ticha krinsky
$$: all major credit cards accepted
dinner. wine. reservations recommended

midtown > e45

atlanta is a hilly city with streets that arc and wind east to west, north to south. every time i thought i might be a bit lost, i'd stumble upon someplace where i wanted to be. that's how i ended up at *tierra*. first the yellow of the exterior caught my eye here, then i recognized the name, and within minutes i'd met ticha and dan and was eating their delectable cuisine of the americas. *tierra's* cuisine is not a fusion hodge-podge but instead a menu of enticing entrees that are delegates, if you will, of their respective countries.

imbibe / devour:
montgras reserva merlot, chile
02 broquel cabernet sauvignon argentina
black bean soup with apple-cured bacon,
    platanos fritos & crème fraiche
mussels in pasilla pepper broth
sauteed halibut in trinidadian tamarind sauce
churrasco tipico salvadoreño
awesome tres leches cake

99

toast

casual new american cuisine with southern accents

817 west peachtree st northeast, suite e-125. between sixth and cypress
404.815.3033 www.toastrestaurant.com
brunch sun 11a - 3p lunch mon - fri 11:30a - 2:30p
dinner tue - thu 5:30 - 10p fri - sat 5:30 - 11p

opened in 2005. owner: thom williams chef: nancy degnan smith
$ - $$: all major credit cards accepted
brunch. lunch. dinner. full bar. catering. reservations recommended

midtown > **e46**

in this day and age when you meet somebody that seems unhurried and relaxed, you have to wonder if that person is just naturally calm or if they hold a secret that the rest of us hassled and harried folk just don't have? i think that thom and nancy know the secret, and the way that they are going to share it with you is if you visit them at their oasis of mellow, *toast*, which sits in the midst of midtown's skyscrapers. sit down, have a glass of wine and delve into a chicken pot pie. see now, don't you feel better?

imbibe / devour:
woodchuck amber cider
torbreck woodcutters semillion
lemon tarragon chicken salad
crab cakes
chicken pot pie
chilled beef tenderloin salad
seasonal fruit pie
new orleans bread pudding

toscano & sons italian market

friendly neighborhood grocery store with disctinctive italian flavors

1000 marietta street northwest #106. corner of howell mill road
404.815.8383 www.toscanoandsons.com
mon 10a - 6p tue - fri 10a - 7p

opened in 2006. owners: kathy boehmer and john reed
$ - $$: all major credit cards accepted
lunch. grocery. first come, first served

westside > **e47**

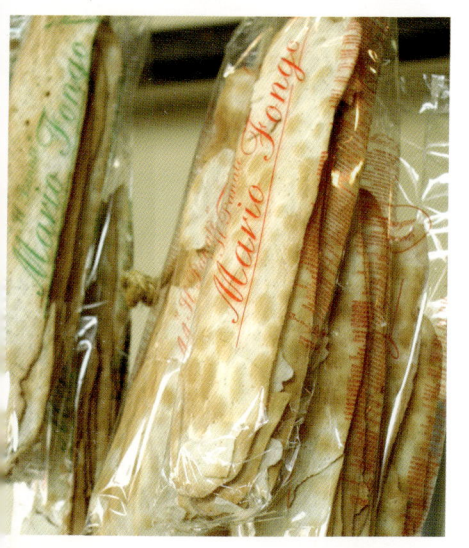

kathy and john bring an authentic taste of old italy to this corner of atlanta. with homemade pastas, olive oils, cheeses, breads, sardines, olives—this is the place where atlantans learn there's more to italian food than chef boyardee. named after kathy's grandfather, *toscano & sons* is truly a neighborhood grocery, featuring carefully selected italian staples and a delicious (no substitutes, please) panini menu. the toscana, my favorite, i prefer "cru" or unpressed, all the better to enjoy its salty goodness. this is my staple. what's yours?

imbibe / devour:
bisson ciliegiolo rosé
rosa del golfo primitivo
abbamele (sardinian honey & pollen reduction)
bono novella unfiltered olive oil
pizza to take home & heat
toscana panini cru
fresh pasta

wasabi

sushi, wine and sake lounge

180 walker street southwest, suite c. between stonewall and haynes
404.574.5680 www.wasabiatl.com
lunch tue - fri 11:30a - 2p dinner mon - thu 5 - 11p fri - sat 5 - midnight

opened in 2006. owners: benjamin krause and nhan v le chef: nhan v le
$ - $$: mc. visa
lunch. dinner. full bar. sushi classes. reservations recommended

castleberry hill arts district > e48

when nhan presents you with any array of sushi, you know it's no coincidence that *wasabi* is located in the arts district. this is a place where they've taken a visual food like sushi and put their own highly artistic and creative spin on it. with names like cherry blossom, pink lady and candy bo—each sushi offering is a delectable work of art. and the cocktails get equal creative consideration. envision, if you will, the party of flavors within a glass of the cucumber ginger sake sangria. can you taste it? i did, and it was so very, very good.

imbibe / devour:
wasabi martini
cucumber ginger sake sangria
mojito de asia
seared albacore with ponzu dressing
chef choice sashimi appetizer
shrimp basil roll
stackedd roll
unagi don

west egg cafe

wholesome comfort food cafe

1168a howell mill road. corner of 14th
404.872.3973 www.westeggcafe.com
mon - fri 7a - 4p sat - sun 8a - 4p

opened in 2004. owner: jennifer johnson chef: patric bell
$ - $$: all major credit cards accepted
breakfast. brunch. lunch. coffee / tea. treats. first come, first served

westside midtown > e49

were you into twinkies or devil dogs as a kid? if you were like me and loved devil dogs and haven't seen one in a dog's age—run, don't walk, to *west egg cafe* and get a whoopie pie, which is pretty close to my beloved devil dog. eating one was like having a memory in my mouth but better because i started my meal by eating dessert first. that never happened when i was a kid! follow up the whoopie pie with a coca cola cupcake, and zowie, you've got yourself the meal of champions.

imbibe / devour:
frozen dancing goat frappé
old-fashioned oatmeal with fruit compote
fried green tomatoes
roast pork loin sandwich with onion marmalade
turkey meatloaf
whoopie pie!!!!!
coca cola cupcakes

zennubian 7 teahouse

organic teahouse featuring organic, vegan and vegetarian food

163 peters street southwest. between spring and trinity
404.521.9961 www.zennubian7teahouse.com
tue - fri 10a - 10p sat - sun 11a - 10p

opened in 2006. owner / chefs: miftah f. ali and noble ali
$ - $$: all major credit cards accepted
breakfast. lunch. dinner. tea. movie and music nights. private parties
first come, first served

castleberry hill arts district > e50

i do truly believe the saying that "you are what you eat." so i like to eat food that is beautifully prepared, tasty and good for me. at *zennubian 7 teahouse*, miftah has all these areas covered. every tea, tonic and entree will have your body singing "yes, that's exactly what i needed" and your taste buds shouting "yes, that's the flavor i was craving." for those carnivores who feel a bit put-off with the whole vegan/vegetarian thing, i say relax and put yourself in miftah's capable hands and experience a little clean eating.

imbibe / devour:
elixer tonics
healing herbs
white rose zennubian blend tea
pu-ehr tea
nubian noodle bowls
mamma earth salad
tropical spring roll dessert

notes

eat

shop

1*five*0

a lifestyle fusion of great things
1000 marietta street northwest, #104. corner 8th
404.474.4102 www.150atlanta.com
mon - sat 11a - 7p

opened in 2007. owners: lanny west, leslie fram and jennifer ripley
all major credit cards accepted
everything is less than $150!

midtown > **s01**

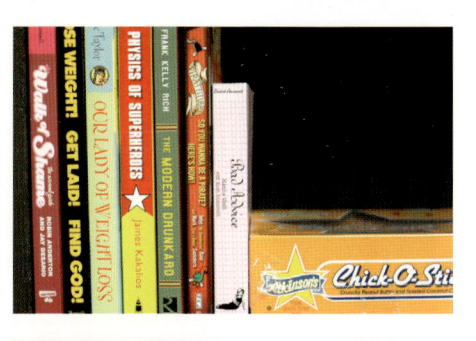

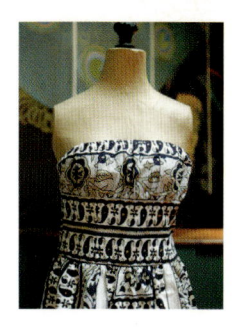

have you ever gone out, with a pocket full of mad money looking for a special treat and been unable find a single thing to buy because everything was just too frickin' expensive? you'll never have that problem at *1*five*0* as everything, and i mean everything, here is under 150 clams. this general store is filled to the rafters with unusual, of-the-minute fashions for men and women, gifts, home accessories, books and vintage candies. whatever your mood, whatever your shopping need, you're bound to find exactly what you didn't know you were looking for at prices that won't break the bank.

covet:
goorin brothers fedora
quail balloon skirts
hanna jo eyelet cotton tunics
seychelles red patent leather flats
assorted men's vintage snap western shirts
outfit printed totes
vintage candy

20th century antiques

antiques and decorative accessories

1054 north highland avenue northeast. between north virginia and los angeles
404.874.7042 www.20thcenturyantiques.net
daily 11a - 7p

opened in 1983. owners: vic matich and lance kern
all major credit cards accepted
online shopping

virginia · highland > **s02**

i was immediately drawn into *20th century antiques* because i couldn't get over how many items there were that i coveted. this wasn't just an assortment of any old pieces but choice designs spanning the last hundred or so years that i personally wanted or knew somebody who would. i could see the snakeskin footstool in my living room and i knew exactly who would like the framed butterflies. but the trip through time that i really enjoyed was finding the edition of life magazine from my birth week. that's an amusing little time capsule anybody would cherish.

covet:
life magazines (find your week of birth)
mies van der rohe for knoll orange chair
stainless steel jorge pensi-inspired chair
the fine art board game
coral lampshade bag
framed butterflies species
wicker victorian beach chair
vintage fabric

beehive co-op

one-stop shopping for locally designed goodies
1831a peachtree road northwest. between palisades and 28th
404.351.1166 www.beehiveco-op.com
mon - fri 11a - 7p sat 10a - 7p

opened in 2004. owners: petra geiger
all major credit cards accepted
online shopping. craft workshops. classes. custom orders / design

buckhead > s03

what's all the buzz about at *beehive co-op*? let me tell you. there's a bit of a chic, modern-day antique mall feeling here, though instead of antiques dealers, the vendors are local designers creating everything from stylish shoes to stationery, and from colorful baby clothes to pillows. even though it was april, visions of my christmas gift list danced in my head. *beehive* is the perect one-stop shopping experience: something for me, something for friends and family, something for me. and i can buy all this without the fear of being stung by sticker shock—joy to the world!

covet:
tasha hussey cream linen dress with torch lily
rinse beauty products
love your mama body products
petit parisiens enfant sleeping bag
beau beaux inc. children's clothing
felix kniaznev happy house ceramic miniature notes, ink cards
whimsy press gift wrap, cards & journals

belvedere

exceptional high-end vintage and modern home furnishings and jewelry

996b huff road northwest. between howell mills and boyd
404.352.1942 www.belvedereinc.com
tue - sat 11a - 5p

opened in 1998. owner: julia-carr bayler
all major credit cards accepted
online shopping. custom orders / design

westside midtown > **s04**

belvedere is a prominent name from my upper west side childhood in manhattan. it's the name of the castle in central park and also the name of a glorious, stately apartment building overlooking the park. in fact, 'belvedere' means building (or part of a building) offering a fine view of a surrounding area. so when i entered *belvedere* in atlanta, i immediately conjured up my imaginary central park west pied à terre, and then it wasn't hard to make the leap to furnishing it (and myself) with some of the chic offerings from the very real *belvedere*.

covet:
belvedere:
  lucite based lamp
  embroidered pillow
ray augousti shagreen vase
kuk-may embroidered pillow
steve vaubel gold vermeil jewelry
l. frank 18k gold tube bead necklace
esque design water jugs

119

blabla

hand-knit children's apparel, dolls and accessories

1186 virginia avenue northeast. corner of rosedale
404.875.6496 www.blablakids.com
mon - fri 10a - 6p sat 10a - 4p

opened in 2006. owner: susan pritchett, florence wetterland and joseph strong
all major credit cards accepted
online shopping. gift registries. gift baskets. classes. events

virgina - highland > **s05**

part of the *eat.shop* experience is taking the time to stop and chat with the different business owners you meet along the way. often, thanks to these impromptu chit-chats, i learn about newly opened or off-the-beaten-path places. *blabla* was both of these. i had photographed their fantastic knit toys and kids' clothing numerous times in other cities but i had no idea the company was based in atlanta. that is until the owner of *knitch* told me about *blabla's* brand new shop. i was thrilled. and i must say in this case, the gift of gab goes a long way.

covet:
blabla
  bubbles knit doll
  knit rattles
  kooka finger puppet set
  orange cat & butterfly knit backpacks
  basil vest
  cloud cardigan
  blue/green striped chinese pants

121

city issue

vintage and classic modern furnishings and accessories

2825 peachtree street northeast. corner of rumson
404.262.3500 www.cityissue.com
mon - tue noon - 5p thu - sat 11a - 6p

opened in 2001. owner: jennifer sams
mc. visa
monthly inventory updates via email. online shopping. custom orders

buckhead > **s06**

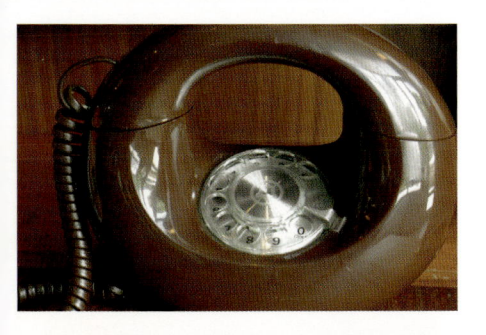

back in the seventies my mom bought my dad one of those clackety-clack e,xecutive desktop toys. do you remember the four attached columns, with the stainless steel balls hanging from clear nylon? you took one, pulled it back, and then it rythmically hit the others... clackety-clack, clack, clack. thirty years later, here at *city issue*, i see the donut phone and a knoll walnut and steel desk, and the memory of playing at my father's desk comes back to me. that's the beauty of it here: you can feel the presence of the past, but you want to buy everything to make it a part of your future.

covet:
'60s paul mccobb bar by calvin
tom van hosen pixel artwork
vintage bamboo serving tray
'70s westinghouse donut phone
'60s teak desk with floating top
paul volther chair by frem rojle
holmegaard glassware

dresscodes

defining style for men and women

201 west ponce de leon avenue, #117. corner of commerce, to the side of artisan blvd
404.343.2894 www.dresscodesatl.com
sun 11:30a - 6:30p mon - wed 11:30a - 7:30p thu - sat 11:30a - 8:30p

opened in 2007. owners: karen and brett mascavage
all major credit cards accepted
online shopping. custom orders / design

decatur > s07

karen and brett are style mixologists. what is this exactly? it's when you take a dash of art, some sleek clothing lines, and you mix these two with a bit of big city culture (both are transplanted new yorkers) and what you get is their stylish clothing salon, *dresscodes*. if you're into denim like i am, this is a great place to find the good stuff. there are several brands here of the over-dyed indigo, selvage variety. pair these with slim shirts and vintage t's and you've got a look that is not only perfect for atlanta but for just about anywhere you choose to be.

covet:
5ep men's japanese selvage denim
slings & stone free-trade denim
rogues gallery nautical t's
corpus jeans & tops
yoko devereaux henley
borne shirt dress
aem'kei skirt
soia & kyo grey herringbone jacket

eco-bella

organic lifestyle boutique

1046 north highland avenue. between north virginia and los angeles
404.815.4280 www.eco-bella.com
mon - wed 10a - 7p thu - sat 10a - 9p sun noon - 6p

opened in 2006. owner: antje kingma
all major credit cards accepted
online shopping. gift registries. gift baskets. custom orders / design. monogramming

virginia - highland > s08

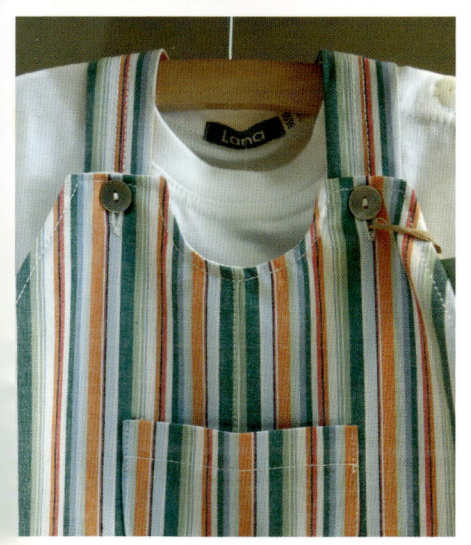

i've been branching out and integrating more and more organic products into my life. though i'm committed to the environment, i want the products i use to also be stylish, and this is where *eco-bella* comes into the picture. from house paint to bathrobes, baby clothes to bedding, *eco-bella* is one-stop shopping for everyday items that are both designed well and good for you and the environment around you. there's no scratchy, hippy hemp-sack dresses here, just a great assortment of choice organinic options for every aspect of your life. it's easy being green.

covet:
anna sova linens, towels & house paints
nandina bamboo towels
lana women's & infant wear
kate quin infant wear
erba viva skincare
bleubay candles
dream designs pillows & bedding
speesees women's & infant wear

elements of style

a boutique and gallery of wearable art

258 pharr road northeast. between peachtree and north fulton
404.846.2182 www.elementsofstyleatl.com
tue - sat 11a - 5p or by appointment

opened in 2006. owner: nancy lowe turner
all major credit cards accepted

buckhead > **s09**

there are clothing designs out there that are so contrived they require a user's manual and attendants to put on. then there is the wearable art you will find at *elements of style*. this clothing is simple in its essence, but through manipulation of fabric, a piece may seem to defy gravity, capture or reflect light and drape the figure just so. this is not the type of clothing for label lemmings but instead for women who are interested in looking like no one else. and the cool thing is, just one piece from here will transform even something as mundane as a pair of jeans into a special look.

covet:
lynn mizono asymetric clothing
ray harris clothes
mashiah arrive pleated bolero
babette black pleated blouse
janet kaneko vintage handbags
rafael sanchez leather embellished handbag
patricia von musulin lucite cuff

form

an emporium of the unexpected

2165 college avenue. corner of murray hill
404.370.1266 www.formdesigngroup.com
mon - sat 8a - 9p sun 9a - 9p

opened in 2003. owner: max leblanc and alison lueker
all major credit cards accepted
gift registries. gift baskets. custom orders / design. interior design

historic kirkwood > s10

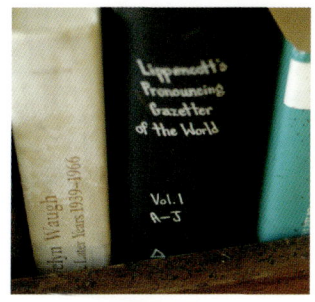

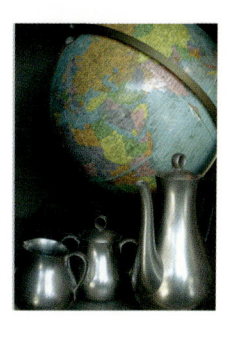

because of my love of history, good design and high craftsmanship, i enjoy seeing old, once abandoned buildings reimagined into vibrant, new buildings. love, love, love. so when i pulled up to the beautifully restored hardware store that houses *form* (and *sun in my belly*) i was close to tears of joy. once inside, the joy was amplified. every object here seems like it was handpicked to honor its unique shape and function, and be useful. i wanted everything i touched, and i probably touched everything in sight. good form, max!

covet:
form vintage fabric pillows
paddy wax candles
leather club chairs
1953 flair magazine
boat porthole folding table
snow & graham letterpress cards
walter anderson woodcut prints

frock of ages

twentieth century vintage fashion

1653b mclendon avenue northeast. between page and clifton
404.370.1006 www.frockofages.com
wed - sat noon - 6p sun noon - 4p

opened in 1990. owner: karen kennedy
mc. visa
online shopping

candler park > **s11**

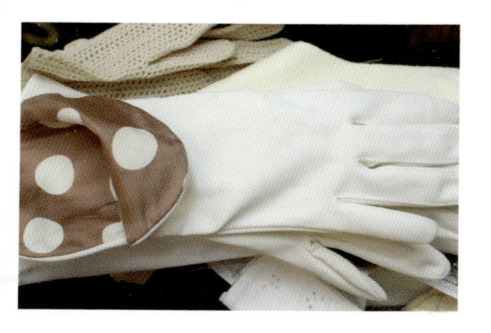

my first babysitting money splurges were on a '30s chiffon-y, garden party dress and a pink satin bed jacket that i would wear with army fatigues, much to the confusion of my parents. i've been collecting vintage ever since. when my friend marcia brought me to *frock of ages,* i was so enraptured with karen's selection, marcia had to leave me there and come back later, much later. this is one big, carefully edited boudoir: floor to ceiling hats and handbags, trays and trays of jewelry and wall-to-wall fashion history. if the clothes and accessories in this store could talk, the stories they would tell...

covet:
'60s two-piece swimsuits
cream ribbon cardigan
hand-painted silk kimono
'30s yellow floral chiffon garden dress
early 20th century cotton dress with ruffle hem
sheer print shirt dress
wood bead bag
gold mesh clasp bracelet

133

kaleidoscope boutique featuring 4bags

colorful co-ed emporium

252 west ponce de leon avenue. corner of ponce de leon
404.378.1214 www.kscopeboutique.com
mon noon - 6p tue - wed 10a - 7p thu - sat 10a - 9p sun noon - 5p

owner: camille wright
all major credit cards accepted

decatur > s12

remember the visual sensation you used to have as a kid when you put you looked into a kaleidoscope? it was a carnival of color and shifting shapes. i can understand why this colorful co-ed emporium is called *kaleidoscope*. everywhere your eye looks there's a spectrum of different pattern and color combinations. camille sources near and far for hip, current clothes for all occasions from chic workplace attire to nightclubbin' duds. there's a prism of possibilities here to brighten up your wardrobe.

covet:
tasha hussey dresses
collective clothing houndstooth chiffon dress
noltia sundress
lu lu lamé dress
modern amusement shorts
ben sherman shirts & ties
triple 5 soul pork pie hats

knitch

an inviting, inspiring world of knitting

1052 saint charles avenue. corner of federica
404.745.9276 www.shopknitch.com
mon - fri 10:30a - 7p sat - sun 10:30 - 6p

opened in 2006. owner: kim nickels
all major credit cards accepted
online shopping. gift registries. classes. custom orders / design

virgina · highland > **s13**

i have a theory about the knitting craze that has swept the nation. as we advance technologically and spending more and more time working in isolation at the computer or glued to tivo, humans, as social beings, still crave and thrive on interaction. and we also appreciate things made by hand. hence the attraction to the crafts of old—creative, tactile cures for what's ailing us. for this type of medicine, stop by knitch. where you'll find luxurious yarn, great knitting tools and good conversation. a warm, inviting community exists here, and you'll feel better the moment you step inside.

covet:
material whirld one-of-a kind art yarns
habu textiles
suss cousins yarns
be sweet mohair (s. african job creation program)
the fiber company organic yarns
beadie's handmade knitting beadles
claudia handpaints handpainted yarns
be sweet hook loom knitting bags

137

little sparrow floral design

artisanal flowers

1185 virginia avenue northeast. corner of rosedale
404.249.8366 www.littlesparrowflowers.com
tue - sat 10a - 6p

opened in 2004. owner: susan sleeper
all major credit cards accepted
gift baskets. classes. custom orders / design. wedding specialists

virgina · highland > s14

little sparrow floral design is like a mini art gallery where nature's shapes and colors form works of art. be it one heroic lily or a round of grass that is surrounded by other greens—susan has a way of mixing the different elements together as if she were wielding a brush dipped in colorful paint. in fact, she'll actually frame densely placed clusters of different flowers in compositions ready to hang on a wall. a framed garden—how ingenious. i think monet would be a bit jealous!

covet:
bumblebee lavender
astilbe
fritillaria
orchids
stalks of okra
little sparrow art gallery

lui-b

made-to-measure (and ready-to-wear) italian shirts
1116 west peachtree street northwest. between 12th and 13th
404.810.0031 www.lui-b.com
tue - fri 11a - 6p sat noon - 5p

opened in 2003. owner: melinda chandler
all major credit cards accepted
online shopping. custom orders / design

midtown > s15

savile row is famous for bespoke suits, but in italy, "camiceria," the craft of made-to-measure shirting, is the name of the game. *lui-b* brings this specialty to atlanta, and the word is spreading. men (or the women who shop for them) can now select the collar, cuff, fit and fabric of their dress shirts. what was once an unattainable luxury is accessible, thanx to melinda. whether you choose custom-made or ready-to-wear shirting, each piece of clothing is hand made in a small town outside bologna, assuring the quality loses nothing in translation while crossing the continents.

covet:
shirting:
  blue & white windowpane check
  green, brown & white tattersall
  white poplin shirt
  pronto: executive shirts on-call!
black & grey houndstooth silk tie
paisley pocket square

luxe

affordable exclusivity
1000 marietta street northwest, #102. corner of 8th
404.815.7470 www.luxeatlanta.com
mon - sat 11a - 7p

opened in 2007. owners: lanny west, leslie fram and jennifer ripley
all major credit cards accepted

westside midtown > **s16**

there is a limit to what i'll pay for designer threads. even if the item of clothing is "worth it," once past a certain decimal, it falls into the "emperor's new clothes" territory for me. at *luxe*, whether the clothing be designer, couture or vintage, you'll find discounts up to 80%. this puts some fun (and reality) back into fashion aquisitions. if you pause, like i do, for the three m's: marc jacobs, missoni and marni—come on down; you'll find them all represented here. this is the new "price is right" where you can indulge in guilt-free buying without fear of a scolding from your accountant.

covet:
missoni plaid coat
marc jacobs jersey wrap dress
hogan raffia bag
sheri bodell sahara minidress
vivo shagreen cuff
loona paris grey jersey dress
estate jewelry

143

mooncake

vintage-inspired, yet modern fashion and jewelry

1019 virginia avenue northeast. corner of north highland
404.892.8043 www.mooncakeboutique.com
mon - sat 11a - 7p

opened in 1979. owner: janet armell
all major credit cards accepted

virgina · highland > **s17**

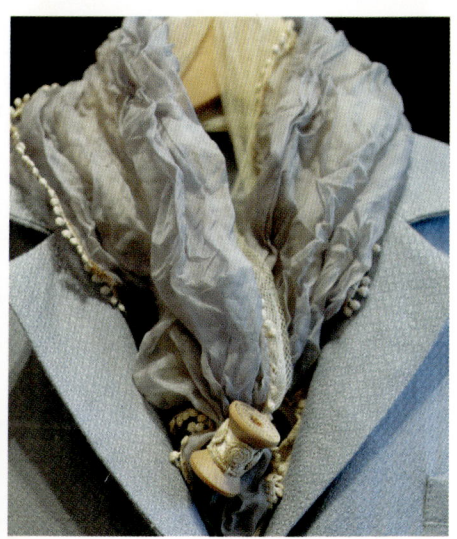

do you remember the when you first heard the term, "new romantics?" it was probably in the early '80s when you were obsessed with watching spandau ballet on mtv. the clothes from this era were theatrical, to say the least. now in the new century you can find a totally modern "new romantic" style at *mooncake*. the vintage-inspired clothing here is utterly wearable and beautifully made. so if you're looking to make yourself look and feel a bit more romantic, just step over the threshold into the world of *mooncake*.

covet:
lilith of paris waistcoat
trelise cooper jacket
rozae nichols dress
viviana uchitel '20s inspired dress
calleen cordero leather vest
rundholz antiqued white skirt & jacket
beth ordun jewelry
elisa ferare black suede & snake wedge

o'clair de lune

fine european lingerie

322 peters street southwest, suite four. corner of mcdaniel
404.681.6644 www.oclairdelune.com
by appointment only

opened in 2006. owner: lamia aouassi
all major credit cards accepted
online shopping. gift registries. gift baskets

castleberry hill art district > **s18**

except for valentine's day or bridal showers, americans are really behind (excuse the pun) when it comes to lingerie. some department stores still refer to the lingerie area as "foundations." where's the intrigue there? thankfully, lamia at *o'claire de lune*, armed with her french appreciation for all things luxurious and an exclusive stash of gorgeous european lingerie, shows atlantans how to work "under-luxe" into daily life. you'll want to lounge around day and night in these delicate pretties, but trust me, when you finally do get dressed, you'll exude a certain *je ne sais quoi*!

covet:
assia lingerie
huit jolie poupee lingerie
ravage tanga collection
princess tam tam ombrelle chemise
simone perele florence collection
cotton club lingerie
guia la bruna charming doll nightgown

olive

vintage-inspired dresses, separates and bridal

442 east paces ferry road northeast. between east shadowland and maple
404.274.5432 www.olivestyle.com
by appointment

opened in 2001. owner: katriesa raines
all major credit cards accepted
online shopping. gift registries. custom orders / designs

buckhead > s19

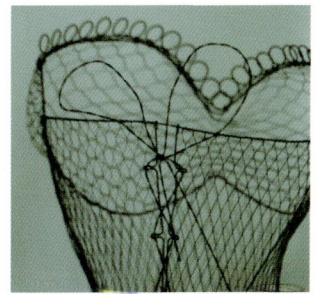

the sculptural silhouettes of the '50s and '60s have enduring appeal because they are feminine, flattering and forgiving. ever look through family albums at pictures of your mom, aunt or gran? the '80s: cringe. '70s: roll eyes and guffaw. but the late '50s and early '60s: cry misty for me because the ladies looked great. katriesa obviously knows her fashion history; she keeps her silhouettes at *olive* simple and her fabrics fancy. this way, all figures are flattered, with nothing to distract, so years from now when you see photos of yourself, you'll still think you looked great.

covet:
katie strapless cocktail dress
emily front pleat skirt
beatrice two-pocket skirt with banding
abigail dress
libby collarless jacket
olive trunk shows catered by chef angela!

149

pollen

creative flowers and unusual wares

432 east paces ferry road northeast. corner of east shadowlawn
404.262.2296 www.pollenatlanta.com
tue - sat 10a - 5p sat 11a - 4p

opened in 1999. owners: bonnie garrison and chris condon
all major credit cards accepted

buckhead > s20

other than my springtime birthday, i have always dreaded the season due to my lifelong struggle with pollen allergies. ahhh, pollen—what i wouldn't do to have a better relationship with you. drugs haven't worked, nor have homeopathic remedies. but wait! is there hope for me to have a good relationship with this pesky sneezing agent? yes, there is, as long as it's the wonderful nursery named *pollen*. here i can happily sniff the beautiful flowers and treat myself to beautifully designed products—here, i'm allergic to nothing other than the idea of going broke buying everything in sight.

covet:
specialty posies
campo di fiori
sweet bella cards
alex marshall pottery
hable bags & pillows
j. schwartz birdfeeders & houses
handmade chinese faux bois
robert ogdon handcrafted found-object lamps

providence antiques

antiques and so much more

1409 n highland avenue northeast. corner of university
404 872 7551 www.providenceantiques.com
mon 11a - 6p tue - thu 11a - 9p fri sat 11a - 10p sun noon - 6p

opened in 1992. owner: claudia thompson
all major credit cards accepted
online shopping. custom orders/design. interior design consultations

morningside > s21

when i entered *providence antiques*, i was immediately won over by claudia's charming and unique juxtapositioning of global antiques, art and contemporary lifestyle products. i felt right at home here; so much so, that i fantisized it was my home where i would slip into the house inc. voile tunic then decide where to hang one of the 19th century portraits available, and then find a good spot for the beaded fez and finally ponder what summertime treat i'd serve in the depression glassware bowls. so much to figure out and so little time before claudia realizes i've moved in.

covet:
assorted paintings & etchings
robin's egg soap
house inc. voile tunic
small demi-john bottles
large blood coral pieces
colorful felt pet toys
hypotrochoid art set
vintage handpainted ribbon

153

savvy snoot

urban eclectic consignment home furnishings

1187 howell mills road northwest. between huff and 14th
404.355.1399 www.savvysnoot.com
mon - sat 10a - 5p

opened in 2004. owner: marty mason
all major credit cards accepted
custom orders / design

westside midtown > s22

smart folks know that one person's discard is another's treasure. because there's always someone ready to purge, marty is there ready and willing to accept; that is, if the item or items catch his eye and are of great quality. here at *savvy snoot*, consignment no longer means a jumbled array of this and that. here you'll find a wide variety of styles and eras, all carefully chosen, in great condition, and at a nice price. fancy a jolt of chinoiserie with your moderne décor but don't want to break the bank? then this is your type of place.

covet:
chinese-painted desk with bamboo trim
striped turkish rug
baker chinoiserie bar
leather armchairs
bent wood armchair
glass based lamp
wood and stainless steel table & benches
chinoiserie painted screen

skate escape

skateboards, inline skates, bikes and ice cream!
1086 piedmont avenue northeast. corner of 12th
404.892.1292 www.skateescape.com
daily 11a - 7p

opened in 1979. owners: bob orlowski and janice phillips
all major credit cards accepted
online shopping. custom orders. gift certificates. rentals

midtown > **s23**

atlanta has many great parks dotted throughout its neighborhoods. one of my favorites is piedmont park, which was designed with a little help from the famous olmsted brothers. here, people gather for numerous activities including walking through the beautiful botanical gardens, seeing concerts and of course boarding, in-line skating and cycling on the main road through the park. *skate escape*, which faces the 12th street gate, is the place to get geared up to do this, whether you want to buy or just rent. strolling is fun, but rolling is better.

covet:
sk8boards:
  zero
  element
  enjoi
riedell rollerskate boots
electra bikes
fuji bikes
nestle's king ice cream cone

south of market

rustic french antiques, lighting and accessories

1044 north highland avenue northeast. between north virginia and los angeles
404.844.0884 www.southofmarket.biz
mon - thu 11a - 8p fri - sat 11a - 9p sun noon - 6p

opened in 2007. owner: kay douglass
all major credit cards accepted
online shopping

virgina · highland > **s24**

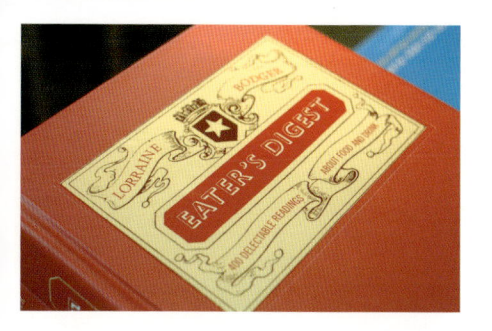

there's something about re-purposing industrial items into functioning, domestic pieces that i've always loved. for example, taking an old zinc bucket and making it into a light is brilliant. i will fess up that i pretty much loved every single item in *south of market*. but what really stopped me in my tracks was kay's unerring use of scale. each piece seemed just this side of oversized so as to give even the simplest cement planter or glass beaker a heroic sensibility. *south of market* is covet central.

covet:
silver cart table
zinc bucket light
raki pottery
brown botanical illustrations
chester sofa
a.s.a. salt & pepper grinder
great books

sprout

stylish children's store

1198 howell mill road. corner of huff
404.352.0864 www.sprout-atlanta.com
mon - sat 11a - 7p sun noon - 5p

opened in 2002. owner: rachel baba
all major credit cards accepted
gift registries. gift baskets. custom orders / design

westside midtown > s25

sprout is more that just a children's store—it's a chic store where you'll purchase things that will create a lifetime of memories. i vividly remember all of the marimekko and florence eiseman pieces that i had in childhood. the bold and playful patterns from these designers made a lasting impression on me and still inform my tastes today. here at *sprout*, you'll find designs by makie and others that are this century's gold standard. most of the things here are so cool, your kids may still be clinging on to stuff when they're packing to head to college.

covet:
makie everything
caramel baby & child
julie arkell paper mâché toys
petit ateau pj's & underwear
zid zid kids blankets, poufs & slippers
vilac tractor & wooden tops
haba wooden toys
dwell bedding for cribs & children

standard

cutting edge, collectable urban streetware

1841 peachtree road northeast. between palisads and 28th
404.355.1410 www.standardatl.com
mon - thu noon - 9p fri - sat noon - 11p

opened in 2003. owner: farshad arshid
all major credit cards accepted
online shopping. custom orders / design

buckhead > **s26**

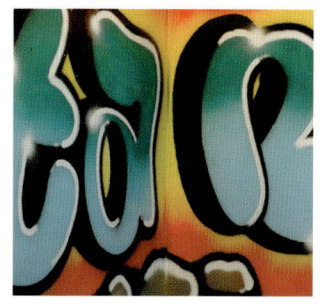

i have been collecting maharishi dpm pieces since my friend hardy starting this military/utilarian inspired line in the early '90s. his hybrid inspiration of indian/yoga/martial arts/military themes make for cool, comfortable and collectable clothing. any store that carries maharishi dpm is ok in my book, and *standard* goes well beyond just ok as this is a archival sneaker-freaker-fiender's paradise. added bonus, *standard* stays open late friday and saturday nights, so you can get your swerve on before you get your swerve on!

covet:
maharishi dpm!!!
g-star
bbc ice cream hoodies
10 deep
mcq
cantiva hempfiber
nike air zoom dunkesto
nike air woven footscape x clot

stefan's

men's and women's vintage

1160 euclid avenue northeast. corner of moreland
404.688.4929 www.stefansvintage.com
mon - sat 11a - 7p sun noon - 6p

opened in 1977. owners: rebecca birdwhistell and tom murphy
all major credit cards accepted

little five points > **s27**

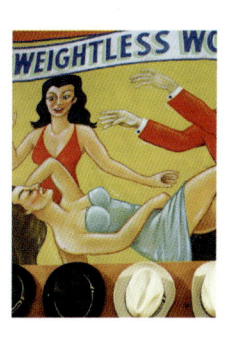

if i could turn back time... i wouldn't. I'm a modern-age gal, but i do like wearing clothing from past eras. *stefan's*, atlanta's oldest vintage clothing store, covers most of the last hundred years or so, so my many dressing moods are satisfied here. '50s cocktail dress? check. '60s pucci prints? check. seersucker or linen suits for the gatbsy in your life? check. i could go on and on as the selection here is that deep, that immaculate. i guess if i could turn back time, i would go back to *stefan's* over and over again.

covet:
pucci long sleeve t-shirt & skirt
yves saint laurent green silk scarf
'30s creme silk velvet evening gown
white linen men's suit
cashmere cardigan
grey mink vest
victorian dresses, blouses & under-skirts

the bilt-house

a little bit of everything in a cozy cottage

511 east paces ferry northeast. corner of maple
404.816.7702 www.thebilt-house.com
mon - sat 9:30a - 6p

opened in 1996. owner: jan bilthouse
all major credit cards accepted
online shopping. gift registries. gift baskets. custom orders / design

buckhead > s28

forget the terrible twos. if ever there were ever a situation fraught with the potential for torture, it would have to be the mother/teenage daughter shopping trip. ok, it's maybe not the worst torture, but it's right up there with a slow-drip faucet. *the bilt-house,* though, has this problem solved. mothers can shop the parlour emporium full of "every day is a vacation" bright fashions and housewares. teens can shop upstairs in the 'tween sanctuary bursting with cool must-haves, not to be heard from again until, with the sweetest voice they can muster, they ask: "mom, can i get this?"

covet:
notice white eyelet tunic
provence quilted
0039 italy shirtdress
betsy johnson raffia flat
nick & mo short velvet fitted jacket
hazel tunic
eyebons reading glasses

167

twelve boutique

unique gift, jewelry and art boutique
860 peachtree street northeast, suite f. between 6th and 7th
404.961.7676 www.twelveatlanta.net
seasonal hours, please call

opened in 1996. owner: john mcdonald
all major credit cards accepted
custom orders / design

midtown > **s29**

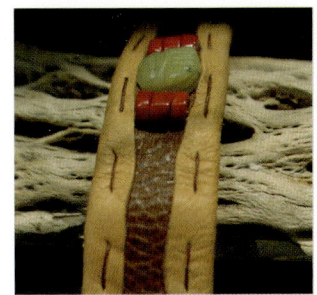

the totem wasn't the first unusual piece that caught my eye at *twelve*, but it was certainly the item that captured my imagination. how was i going to ship it home? where would i put it? should i repaint my living room walls something neutral to offset its vibrant colors? hmm. and i best buy the cowichan knit slippers to wear when i rearrange my furniture to make space for the totem. then i see a gorgeous ebony and zebra wood clutch. do i need another clutch? so many questions. so many desires. my trip to *twelve* had the wheels in my head spinning!

covet:
connie verrusio bent nail bracelet
koo koo design hooded baby towels
monika van schellenbeck earrings
hazelbrand ebony & zebra wood clutch
cowichan knit slippers
kevin peskin open window painting
eieio studio wrapping paper

twelve flowers

sculptural floral

1000 piedmont avenue northeast, suite d. corner of 10th
404.541.2357 www.twelveatlanta.net
mon - fri 9:30a - 7:30p sat 10a - 5:30p

opened in 2005. owner: john mcdonald
all major credit cards accepted
custom orders / design. events. delivery. modern floral design for businesses

midtown > **s30**

while i was shooting at *fune*, i was entranced by a floral arrangement there with its lyrical, floaty orchids juxtaposed against waxy, broad tropical leaves. there was a graphic, yet playful, sensibility to the arrangement, and when i found out the flowers were by john, the owner of *twelve boutique* and *twelve flowers,* it all made sense—especially since part of the triumvirate is *twelve graphics,* a design studio. a-ha! and bravo to john for being a mastermind at filling all of our lives with good design and pretty things.

covet:
purple howard's dream
large white phalaenopsis
exotic lady's slipper
succulents
maidenhair fern
shampoo ginger
hanging heliconia
eremurus

urban cottage

enabling your house to feel like home

3211 cains hill place norhtwest.   between east andrews and irby
404.760.1334   www.urbancottage-atlanta.com
mon - sat   10a - 6p

opened in 1999.   owner: gail a. silverstein
mc. visa
gift registries.   gift baskets.   custom orders

buckhead > **s31**

ever feel the need to turn your city dwelling into the weekend country house of your dreams? urban cottage is the place to come then. here you'll find a stellar assortment of benches, chairs, armoires, hutches, local art, gifts and other useful household items. gail manufactures most of the furniture with her own unique twist, like the wicker spagetti chair which begs to be sat on with a cup of tea and a good book on a lazy sunday. gail has taken country cottage décor and turned it into a cottage industry.

covet:
  urban cottage:
  small & large hutches
  wicker "spaghetti" chair
  striped stained wood dresser
  antiqued white credenza with window pane
 unique cabinet knobs
 portugese ceramics

173

urban fusion

where street meets art

237a peters street southwest. corner of fair
404.653.0222 www.urbanfusionlife.com
mon - thu 11a - 8p fri - sat noon - 9p sun by appointment

opened in 2006. owner: valerie boucher
all major credit cards accepted
online shopping. custom orders

castleberry hill arts district > **s32**

the castleberry hills arts district is percolating. walking down peters street felt a bit like being in soho (nyc) in the early '80s when art galleries sprang up in warehouses and urban culture was pulsating. here there's a variety of high and low art galleries, old-fashioned and newfangled barber shops, bars and restaurants. in the midst of this is *urban fusion*—which perfectly represents the vibrancy of this area. you'll find urban designs here that will represent you well, whether you're walking the streets of atlanta or nyc.

covet:
sneakers:
  creative recreation
  jb classics
  keep
l.a.m.b. everything
anktik denim for boys/girls
hellz bells t's
bijules nyc gold machine gun necklace

175

veruca

independent boutique with hard-to-find labels for men and women

814 juniper street northeast. between 5th and 6th
404.815.9977 www.shopveruca.com
tue - sat 11a - 8p sun noon - 4p

opened in 2005. owner: stefani lidestri
all major credit cards accepted
custom orders

midtown > **s33**

fear not. there is nothing willy wonka-ish about *veruca*. stefani just likes the name *veruca,* and i just like her store. first of all, i love shopping in converted homes and *veruca* is spread out in colorful rooms on the parlour floor of a victorian townhouse—instant cozy feeling. you'll feel so at home here; it's like popping into the house of a friend who just happens to have a wickedly-good wardrobe. and not only are there great women's clothes, there are also men's. ahh, *veruca*, you're a good egg after all.

covet:
super lucky vintage re-constructions
covet eco-fabric garments
union jeans
pecan pie couture t's
becca cowan bou-cou jewelry
roar men's shirts
caffeine men's shirts

victoria's red carpet

shoes and rare accessories from spain

3277d roswell road northeast. between east andrews and alberta
404.731.4502 www.victoriasredcarpet.com
tue - sat 11a - 6p (appointments recommended)

opened in 2006. owner: victoria patón pascual
all major credit cards accepted

buckhead > s34

victoria is doing her civic duty by bringing extraordinary spanish shoes and bold accessories to the good citizens of atlanta. really, this is a community service. the inventory at *victoria's red carpet* changes every three months or so, but the constant is the spectacular styles. i swear, these shoes could walk a red carpet on their own! and you'll never have to worry about seeing your special purchase on zillions of other ladies' feet as victoria stocks only three pairs of each shoe. now that's special

covet:
shoes:
  paco gil
  belen doñate
  blay
victoria patón pascual jewelry:
  bone and wood cuff
  natural pearl bib
  turquoise & coral necklace bib

victory vintage home

exceptional vintage furniture and more

303 east college avenue. corner of trinity and candler
404.373.5511 www.victoryvintage.com
sun - mon noon - 5p tue - sat 11a - 7p

opened in 2004. owner: lee cuthbert
all major credit cards accepted
online shopping. custom orders / design. repairs

decatur > s35

walking into *victory vintage home*, i found myself reflecting on just how much society has changed in the past fifty years. admiring the library card catalog cabinet re-purposed as a coffee table, i thought to myself, "when was the last time i used the dewey decimal system?" hmm, long pause to ponder. well, i always liked the cabinets, and it's sure nice to see them being used again in a creative way. and there are so many other amazing things here that will take you back in time. no doubt you'll find great uses for these things in your world of today.

covet:
robs john gibbings dining chairs
vintage fisher price toys
burke pedestals chairs
pine veneer hanging lamps
card catalog rolling coffee table
vintage 1951 wallpaper samples
vintage pull-down school maps
reisenthal garderobe

wiggle

fresh clothing for girl's and boy's

305 east college avenue. corner of candler
404.373.2522 www.wigglewearkids.com
tue - sat 9a - 5p sun noon - 5p

opened in 2007. owner: kolby sanders-lewis
all major credit cards accepted
online shopping. gift registries. gift baskets
custom orders. in-house monogramming

decatur > s36

"keep still!" growing up, you probably heard that enough to think it was your name. remember when it took practically all of your concentration to keep from bopping around when you were supposed to be standing in line? remember writhing and squirming when you were supposed to be sitting calmly? at *wiggle*, kolby pays homage to those childhood years by providing cool clothes for the itchy-mcfidgets in your life. there's even in-house monogramming just to make it easier to call them by their real names!

covet:
paulina quintana everything
appaman samurai t's
tea collection mediterranean coast dress
angel art bags
babay london recycle vintage fabric
heaven kid's monogrammables
charlie rocket boy's & girl's clothing

young blood gallery & boutique

handmade items from all over the country

629 glenwood avenue southeast. between boulevard and waldo
404.627.0393 www.youngbloodgallery.com
wed and fri noon - 6p thurs noon - 7p sat - sun noon - 5p

opened in 1999. owners: kelly teasley and maggie white
mc. visa

grant park > **s37**

nobody ever said being an artist was easy. in fact, many artists, if queried, would probably say creating art is fulfilling but a mighty struggle. that's why you have to thank people like kelly and maggie, who really believe in supporting young artists and are doing it on a daily basis at *young blood gallery & boutique*. here you'll find the counterculture well represented in everything from posters to re-purposed track jackets. and when you buy something here, you know that you're supporting somebody following his or her dream and that's cool.

covet:
papa studios roadside sign prints
cole gerst print protector
lee marchalonis' flowering trees of appalachia
    illustrated cards
fabricate pillows
bomb pop felt pillows
distilled rose handmade beauty products
holly hue side-zip cardigans & tote bags

185

notes

notes

notes

notes

notes

notes

etc.

the eat.shop guides were created by kaie wellman and are published by cabazon books

eat.shop atlanta was written, researched and photographed by agnes baddoo

editing: kaie wellman   copy editing: lynn king   fact checking: emily withrow
additional production: julia dickey

agnes thx: each and every business in this book. marcia and saturn for their generous hospitality! tasha, jacob, victoria, lamia and jason for sharing their atlanta. the band, little feat, for first inspiring me to love this city. the city of los angeles for invaluable navigational training. kaie for her faith and patience. my family for their love, encouragement and support.

cabazon books: eat.shop atlanta
ISBN-13 978-0-9766534-5-5

copyright 2007 © cabazon books

all rights reserved under international and pan-american copyright conventions. no part of this publication may be reproduced, stored in a retrieval system, or transmitted in any form or by any means, electronic, mechanical, photocopying, recording or otherwise, without prior written permission of the copyright owner.

every effort has been made to ensure the accuracy of the information in this book. however, certain details are subject to change. please remember when using the guides that hours alter seasonally and sometimes sadly, businesses close. the publisher cannot accept responsibility for any consequences arising from the use of this book. the eat.shop guides are not advertorial. each business is chosen to be featured on it's merit.

the eat.shop guides are distributed by independent publishers group: www.ipgbook.com

to find more about the eat.shop guides: www.eatshopguides.com

PRINTED IN SINGAPORE